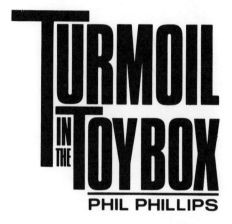

TURMOIL IN THE TOYBOX

PHIL PHILLIPS

TURMOIL IN THE TOYBOX

PHIL PHILLIPS

STARBURST PUBLISHERS

P.O. Box 4123, Lancaster, Pennsylvania 17604

Phil Phillips, evangelist-author, conducts more than 250 multi-media seminars each year on toys, games and cartoons and their effects on children. His video and cassette tapes of the teaching, *The Deception of a Generation,* and newspaper, *Child Affects,* have enjoyed wide distribution throughout the United States, Canada and Australia. Phil has appeared on such shows as *TBN, Contact America, 100 Huntley Street, Marlin Maddoux-Point of View* and *The Hal Lindsey Show.* (For information write: Phillips Ministries, P.O. Box 354, Rockwall, TX 75087.)

Other Books by Starburst Publishers:

The Great Pretender
Devotion in Motion
To My Jewish Friends With Love
You Can Live in Divine Health
A Bucket of Finger Lickin's

Credits

Scripture References: King James Version or Revised Standard Version.

Cover Art by Kernie Erickson.

First Printing, June, 1986
Second Printing, August, 1986
Third Printing, September, 1986

ISBN: 0-914984-04-7
Library of Congress Catalog Number: 86-60428

Printed in the United States of America

I dedicate this book to my parents, Syvelle and Lovie Phillips, who, through their dedication and example, introduced and nurtured me into a relationship with my Heavenly Father.

I also dedicate this book to parents who desire to see their children serve God, parents who are willing to discipline their own lives in order to bring this to fruition.

CONTENTS

INTRODUCTION

In this book, we have sought to make people aware of what is happening today in the toy and cartoon industry. We have tried to show how the occult, violence and heavy sexual overtones in this sort of entertainment are affecting our children.

We not only have taken an in-depth look at the toy and cartoon industry, but also have provided the proper tools needed to assist the reader in the assimilation of that knowledge toward the proper guidance of children, thereby avoiding the "traps" within the media.

There is no way we could thoroughly cover every toy and cartoon series. Such a book would take "volumes." However, let me assure you that *Turmoil in the Toy Box* is the most thoroughly researched and balanced expose available today.

1

UNAWARE

I gasped for breath as the strong fumes from the green, slimy sewage surrounding me forced their way into my throat and nasal passages. Choking and spitting, my three-and-a-half-year-old body struggled to get out of that smelly five-foot deep, five-foot round sewage hole into which I had fallen. Fear began to rise within me as my head bobbed up and down in that awful mess. I tried to call, "Daddy, help me!" but the words would not come. Suddenly, I felt the strong hand of my Dad grab hold of me. With one desperate lunge he pulled me to safety.

This saga began years ago, when my family was traveling in our 32-foot Airstream trailer through the New Mexico-Arizona area. My Dad, who had been a pastor for some years, was now returning to the ministry of "traveling evangelist."

This day we had pulled off the road at a rest stop. It was not a fancy stop—just a dirt place on the side of the road—with outhouses; very crude, not the kind of rest stops we have today. From miles around, all you could see were cactuses.

We stopped the car and got out. Our dog had a great time running around. I, too, was ready to run. I thought I would show my Dad how fast I could run. So, I "set him up" where he could see me. Then, I got into position. Smiling confidently, I backed up, because I thought that was the way to get a better start. I backed up one, two, three, four times.

Suddenly, I heard my father yell, "Look out for the hole!" . . . but it was too late! I was already tipping backward into the sewage that had been dumped there by travelers in trailers. That sewage must have been piling up for some time, because green slime and other refuse were floating around in it.

All I remember about that day was that my Mom and Dad spent the next three hours cleaning me up. There I was, in the middle of the desert with no clothes on, being washed off with the trailer hose.

Today when I speak throughout the country, I liken this experience I had as a child to the plight of many Christians. The intent of their hearts is to please their Heavenly Father, but they are unaware of the "pits" which surround them, pits that contain *spiritual sewage*. They do not seem to sense any danger. In fact, some Christians intentionally "dangle their feet in the mess," thinking that it will not affect their relationship with God. Others "fall" in or "dive" in. The majority of people who fall into the pit are **unaware** that it is there. *This "perishing for the lack of knowledge" hinders many Christians, while sending others into the depths of hell, denying not only the existence of the Father, but also the sewage pit into which they have fallen.*

One way we can avoid pits is to know where they are. Sadly, that does not always keep us from falling into them. We are so drawn to them that we find ourselves in a pit before we know it. One of the "pits" is "sexual immorality," which comes from the thought life. If your thought life is headed toward a "pit" through the "fantasy" realm, via television, movies or literature, then you are more likely to enact those things. (The Lord says that when a man looks on a woman and has lustful desires in his heart, it is sin. Matthew 5:28) Unlike the pit I fell into, the "sewage" from these "pits" enters the mind. ***Sewage of the mind is more difficult to clean out than sewage on the body.*** To be cleansed from it, one needs a renewal of the mind.

"Pits" are not reserved only for adults. Children can also fall into them, just as I did as a child. **Sexually-oriented, occult and violent cartoons are just as bad for children as sexually-oriented, occult and violent television and movies are for adults.** These toys and cartoons form other "pits" into which many children are falling.

I believe the Lord has called me into this ministry to make parents, grandparents and others aware of the truth behind the toys and cartoons which are affecting the lives of today's children.

One of the most important things I tell parents is, *"Your children's relationship to God is as important as your relationship to God. The 'ground is level' at Calvary and God has a vital interest in your child. He wants your child to grow spiritually, just as He wants you to grow spiritually. It does not happen automatically. It takes planting the seed of the Word of God into the heart and watering that ground. Just as you need nourishment from the Word, so your child needs the nourishment he or she receives from your training and example."*

The goal of Christian parents should not be to rear perfect children, but to guide their children to the place where they arrive at adulthood healthy, happy, well-adjusted and spiritually alive. **I have never met a perfect child, but I have met adults who were a tribute to their Godly parents.**

The necessity of reaching children for Jesus at their earliest age cannot be overstated. The Bible says the gospel message is so simple that even a fool can understand. If a fool can comprehend the message of the gospel and experience the saving grace of Jesus Christ, then a child of two or three can comprehend that message.

Despite this, children are being bombarded with toys and

cartoons filled with occult symbolisms. Although many of these toys and cartoons are designed specifically for children, they still are beyond a child's development. One example is *Robotech*, a cartoon, based on a robotic toy, which has 168 episodes, many of which are sexually-oriented.

Many of the occult practices portrayed in cartoons and movies are specifically mentioned in Scripture as being "an abomination to the Lord." It is up to you, the reader, to see that the children whose lives you affect will be protected from the deception of this and future generations.

2

A STARTLING DISCOVERY

Many parents are ignorant of the role toys and cartoons play in a child's life. I was too, until one day when I walked into a toy store.

In October of 1983 I had scheduled two weeks of services, back to back. Before that, my pastor had been teaching on fasting and prayer. He spoke about a sustained "Jewish fast," in which one fasts from sunup to sundown. The Lord had impressed upon me to begin this type of fast during the time that I would be conducting evangelistic meetings; so, I ate mostly vegetables and fruit.

While preaching in Florida, I went to a mall to buy some shaving supplies. After leaving the store, I did something I had not done in years—I walked into a toy store. The first toy I saw was one called *Skeletor*, which was holding a ram's head staff in its hand. I immediately recognized the ram's head as an occult symbol; I decided to buy the toy. I went back to the house and opened the wrapping around the toy. Inside was a little comic book, which I read with astonishment. *"How could any sane person sell this to a child?"* I thought. *It was "loaded," absolutely loaded with the occult from beginning to end.*

After reading the comics and recognizing the occult symbols used, I became even more concerned. *The story in the book was similar to the book of Genesis in the Bible. The only difference was that it was as though Satan, not God, had created the world. Satan's powers ruled not only the bad creatures, but also the good.* That night before ministering to the congregation, I elaborated on what I had discovered in the toy store. Later, I learned that a number of the parents had this toy in their homes and their children were playing with it! I was SHOCKED to learn that these solid Christian parents had so little spiritual discernment.

"I can't believe it!" I said to myself as I settled in my room that night. "Children from this 'Bible-believing' church have occult toys in their homes. If this is the case, then these toys must be in the homes of Christians everywhere."

I had no idea of the extent of this toy series in the marketplace; no idea of the kind of influence it was having on children. It never entered my mind to do something about it. After the service that night, I tossed the toy onto the back seat of my car and forgot about it.

After speaking at three more services in Louisiana, I was driving home to Dallas—trying to make it in one day. If you have ever driven from New Orleans to Shreveport, you know it is a two-lane road most of the way. You usually wind up getting behind some tobacco-chewing fellow in a rusty pickup truck who does not want to go faster than 40 mph. If you do go over 55 mph, you have to be concerned about policemen. If you are stopped for speeding, you are given a ticket of $75, minimum, for doing just a few miles over the speed limit.

I was trying to make the best of this trip, listening to Christian music on the radio and spending time with the Lord. "Out of the blue," the Lord said, "Phil, do you know what happens when children play with a toy?" Understand, He didn't say this in a booming voice; it was more of an inner voice. The Lord and I have a good relationship. He knows that I know how to hear Him.

"No, Lord. What?"

To be truthful, I thought it rather strange that God was talking to me about toys.

Then the Lord said, *"Phil, children project themselves with their imagination into a toy. They give it life, character, abilities and talents and set the surrounding around it. This is how they learn. Through toys like the one you have in the backseat of your car, Satan is gaining control of the minds of millions of children everywhere. I want you to do something about it."*

"Lord, I am an evangelist, not a children's minister."

The Lord spoke many words to me during this very short period of time. It was a tremendous dealing of the Holy Spirit in my life. It was like the day that the Lord called me into the ministry when I was 18 years old. It was such a "shaking" experience. I think it had to be like that because it was a total change of direction for me. In fact, just a few months earlier, the Peters Brothers, who have a ministry concerning "rock music," had offered to give me their slides, set me up, teach me how to make a presentation and give me their excess bookings. However, I did not feel that was what the Lord wanted me to do. Besides, I could not see myself in that type of ministry. So this was a total change of direction for me, like going 180 degrees in a different direction.

When I got home to Dallas, I bought about $25 worth of toys and I read the material that came with those toys. When I spoke at a meeting a few nights later, I told the audience what the Lord had revealed to me. I then read from a *Dungeons and Dragons* brochure, showed them some toys and pointed out some of the occult symbolisms used. That was the beginning of this ministry of proclaiming the truth about toys and cartoons.

For the next five months, I researched toys and cartoons

17

and their effects on children. I produced a slide presentation called *Deception of a Generation*. Subsequently, I began speaking on the subject and showing the slide presentation throughout the country. During this time, my parents were concerned about me because I had sold my car and was living on practically nothing. The expenses from buying projectors and other equipment exceeded the amount I received from supporters; therefore, most of the money used to pay for the ministry came from previous work that I had done, loans from my brother, the sale of my car and many "miraculous happenings."

George, the man who helped me put the slide presentation together, is an unusual and talented man who loves the Lord. I believe my meeting George was ordained by God. George offered to order the equipment I needed because he could get it at wholesale prices. He even used his own money to pay for the equipment and let me pay him whenever I had extra money. This was a miracle!

First, I took photographs of the toys, but they did not turn out well. Then, another friend, a nationally-known photographer, shot some photographs for me—absolutely free. I experienced miracle after miracle of God's provision. Originally, I had been hesitant to ask this friend to shoot the photographs because I knew I would not be able to afford his charges. He is an exceptional photographer, and his photographs were on the cover of *Cycle* magazine for fourteen months in a row.

Unusual things happened during the time he was setting up to shoot the photographs for me—like blown fuses and problems with the camera equipment—things that never before had happened. When he realized what was happening, he called my parents and told them. After praying with them, he went back to work without any problems. It was apparent to us that Satan was trying to keep this ministry from being launched.

Later, when George saw the photographs, his interest in the project increased. The children's pastor at my church also began encouraging me in this ministry. Up until that time, few people saw the importance of what I was saying about toys. Many people thought my ministry was a real joke.

Nevertheless, I was confident that this ministry was ordained by God. Children became an important part of this ministry. I also discovered that children are important to God. In Matthew 18:6,7,10,14, Jesus pronounces a stinging curse on anyone, especially those who believe in Him, who offends a child.

> *But whoso shall offend one of these little ones which believe in me, it were better for him that a millstone were hanged about his neck, and that he were drowned in the depth of the sea.*
>
> *Woe unto the world because of offenses! for it must needs be that offenses come; but woe to that man by whom the offense cometh!*
>
> *Take heed that ye despise not one of these little ones; for I say unto you, That in heaven their angels do always behold the face of my Father which is in heaven.*
>
> *Even so it is not the will of your Father which is in heaven, that one of these little ones should perish.*

God has entrusted children to the care of their parents. He expects parents to guide their children and teach them about the "fruits of the Spirit," which are outlined in Galatians 5:22-23. These include love, joy, peace, patience, gentleness, goodness, faith, meekness and temperance. Before outlining the fruits of the spirit, Paul describes, in verses 19-21, those behaviors that will cause a person to fall from God's grace.

> *Now the works of the flesh are manifest, which are these; adultery, fornication, uncleanness, lasciviousness,*
>
> *Idolatry, witchcraft, hatred, variance, emulations, wrath, strife, seditions, heresies,*

Envyings, murders, drunkenness, revellings, and such like: of the which I tell you before, as I have also told you in time past, that they which do such things shall not inherit the kingdom of God.

A great number of toys on the market today, especially the more popular ones, are based on some of the very ideas, namely witchcraft, idolatry, emulations and murders, that God warns against.

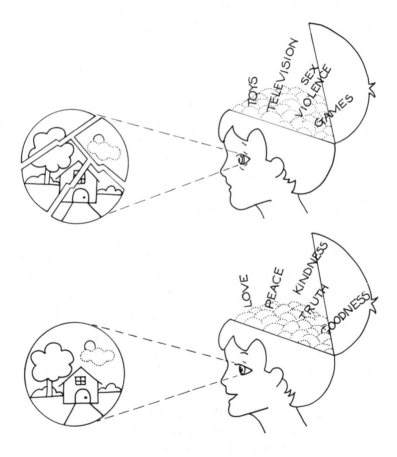

3

LET'S PRETEND

As the Lord had spoken to me earlier, *when a child plays with a toy, he projects his imagination into that toy.* In so doing, the toy becomes an extension of himself. It becomes *real*, just as real as his parents and peers. He assumes close identity with that toy. The subjective nature of the toy, then, is enhanced to unlimited proportions, depending upon the child's interests. Even social scientists recognize that toys are important aspects of the overall environment which shapes a child's moral and social ethics.[1]

Children use play and toys to learn about the world around them. According to Kathy and Mitch Finley in their article *Nurturing Your Imagination,*[2] **a child's mind is like a sponge, soaking up anything and everything it encounters**. The images absorbed become building blocks for making sense out of life and the world. Imagination is closely linked to creativity. Although it is difficult to define, imagination might be described as the ability to ask two questions, "What if?" and "Why not?"[3]

Although imagination is a gift of God, it can be influenced and perverted by outside forces. Those which affect a child's training are parents, toys, television, movies, books and magazines, music, pornography and peer pressure. Actually, parental behavior is the primary influence; however, parents often are "too busy" to spend a great deal of time with their children. As a result, children learn through other sources. These *influences guide a child's imagination. They*

21

form mental images for the child so he can recreate them during his play time and incorporate them into his own life.

Children spend most of their play time in the world of "let's pretend." In his imaginative play, a child can think himself into situations, work out reactions and generally come to terms, his own terms, with people and events.[4] In his imagination, games and play materials are actually miniature replicas of the adult world. He uses these toys, studies them and learns from them. *A child often "visualizes" himself as a certain character, possessing all the attributes and "powers" of that character.* This behavior is often seen when children play "house." They pretend to be adults with a certain "authority" over their "children" (dolls and stuffed animals). This is good, because it lets the child rehearse a role that will later be his. However, *when children consistently pretend to be mystical characters, they are not recreating a real world.* Often, when a person fantasizes too much on one thing, especially on something filled with the occult, that fantasy runs the risk of becoming a reality. Herein lies a problem.

Some "experts" believe fantasy is good, healthy. In fact, many psychologists encourage patients to use fantasy and illusions to deal with personal tragedies or physical or emotional setbacks. Others say to fantasize is wrong. Most psychologists agree that, after personal tragedy, illusions and fantasies are crucial to psychological adjustment; however, the patient must have a firm understanding of reality.

Some influences on the imagination can be a healthy form of teaching for a child. Television and books broaden a child's world by introducing him to places he has never been and people he has never met. Toys allow children to let their imagination run free, unrestricted from pre-set ideas. Nevertheless, these good influences also can be extremely harmful if occult symbols and violence are used. Occult symbols and violence guide a child's imagination into the world of Satan.

If left undisciplined, imagination guided by these evil influences can seed crimes of physical passion and violence.[5] There have been many documented accounts of children (and adults) killing themselves or others as a result of their undisciplined imagination and fantasy playing.

To discipline the imagination, it is wise to avoid television, books and toys which present occult, violent or sexual images. Through these, Satan stimulates one's mind to focus on vain and carnal fantasies. *Imaginative play that is not focused on exploring the real world, but on exploring the mystical world, is called "vain imagination."* When involved in "vain imaginative play," children often exalt themselves above God, by pretending to be characters which they believe to be more powerful than Jesus.

A child's mind is corrupted in a subtle manner. With objects, so "cute and innocent" as toys, children's minds are being filled with images of sex, violence and fear. This is *subtle deception.* It is formed, layer upon layer, until these evil and corrupt images are real to the child.

Parents can prevent *subtle deception* by providing children with healthy images, rather than "unhealthy" ones. For example, concerned adults do not let their children eat only "junk food;" they insist that their children eat well-balanced, nutritional meals. Then, why don't they monitor a child's imaginative play? Perhaps, it is because parents do not realize the harm being done. Although parents cannot have complete control over the images their children "soak up," they can help their children develop good habits and "healthy" tastes early in life.[6]

Parents should set the tone for healthy imaginative play by providing toys which are not linked to pre-set ideas. The child should give the toy life from his own experiences, rather than imitating a cartoon character. To arouse a "healthy" imagination, toys should: promote a constructive expression of feelings, thoughts and ideas; help children relive and clarify their experiences—not conflict with them; and help children feel good about themselves when they do their own thinking.[7]

Although imagination is a healthy and necessary phase of a child's development, too much of it can restrict a child's ability to participate in "social" play—another important phase of childhood. Social play enables children to play with others, learn to adjust to the real world and learn how he relates to the rest of the world.[8] Modern society's emphasis on solitary achievement has permeated through families and is affecting childhood. Children today spend much more time in "solitary" play. They play with toys and recreate television scenes with their toys by using their imagination—but, this is done "alone." In this sense, toys and excessive use of the imagination have contributed to this increase in solitary play.[9]

Contrary to this twentieth-century method of solitary play, play throughout history has predominately been "social." Only the rich were able to afford toys; therefore, children from lower-income families were forced to play with each other. Even though children today spend more time engaging in solitary play, if given the choice, most prefer playing with others.[10]

People have often asked me on how I thought Jesus played when he was a little child. Given the fact that Jesus was not born into a wealthy family, he probably spent a lot of time playing with others, including his brothers. Since Galilee is on the Sea of Galilee, Jesus undoubtedly had a knowledge of the water. We know he liked being near the sea, because at least one of his sermons was spoken from a boat. So I would presume that, as a child, Jesus spent a great amount of time playing near water.

Before we reach adulthood, most of us lose the sense of wonderment that is so characteristic in a child's imaginative play.[11] Sadly, children are losing this sense of wonderment at even younger ages because of the occult symbolisms that are so prevalent in toys and cartoons today. ***By the time the child is a teen, unless his parents have instilled Christian values in him, he will have more knowledge of the occult than he will have of God.*** Hence, all of the child's values and attitudes are affected. Therefore, we now have a generation growing up with attitudes turned against God.

4

THE BRIDGE TO ADULTHOOD

Play—that wonderful world of fantasy, imagination and role playing—is unique to children. Only they can play with blocks and clay for hours without getting bored. We watch in amazement as these little ones recreate the world around them. Sometimes, however, the world they recreate is not so amusing. Then, we wonder if too much play is harmful for a child. It need not be, if closely monitored.

For a child, "play is not mere amusement seeking, but the means by which he gathers information about the world around him."[1] Children must learn how to live in a symbolic and cultural world, seek goals, recognize and respond to meanings of events, people and things, and deal with problems of human relations. Through play, a child, alone or with others, uses toys and games to orient himself to the world and rehearse adult roles.[2]

The foundation for a child's character is laid during his early, formative years. Because preschoolers spend more time in play than in any other activity, researchers claim that the quality and quantity of child's play should not be taken lightly. Instead, they claim play should be regarded as part of the "habit-training and character building" phase of a child's life.[3] Basic attitudes and character traits are learned through specific situations in a child's experience, namely play. Also, children, as well as adults, tend to learn more effectively when doing something they enjoy, rather than by things that are forced upon them by teachings and precepts.[4] Since play is an activity that children enjoy, it does have an effect on their views of the world.

Adults can influence how a child views the world by selecting toys and play material that will help that child grow and learn. Toys should be selected with care because they affect thinking and learning processes. For example, **adults wanting to promote a peaceful society should prohibit war toys. Otherwise, children might learn to believe that all problems are solved through violence, aggression and "conquering a victim."** Likewise, toys that stress or instill fear in a child should be avoided. Children need toys that can be incorporated into their individual "private worlds," finding in them reassurance in an adult world that so often appears strange and even terrifying. As adults, we want children to learn that grownups are warm, friendly and helpful people and that the world is a comfortable, orderly place. Therefore, children should be encouraged to play with dolls, stuffed animals, and engage in dramatic play, because these activities allow children to try new behaviors and learn what it is like to imitate the adults around them.

Through play, a "child lays the foundation for the development of a 'wholesome personality' and the ability to adjust satisfactorily to the world in which he lives."[5] In their play, children learn to figure out how things work. They also learn how to solve problems; develop senses; talk and share ideas; build strength and control of their bodies; develop and express imagination and creativity; about themselves, others and the world; express feelings and energy in healthy ways; and increase ability to concentrate.[6]

If chosen wisely, toys should help promote a "wholesome personality." They should help the child become a "well-rounded individual whose different parts of the personality are fused into a consistent whole, so as to make for the physical and mental health and the social adjustibility of that individual."[7] Remember, a child learns through his environment. Since toys are the primary environment of a child, they play a major role in his mental growth and advancement.

To be the most beneficial to a child's development, toys should meet the following criteria: they should be suitable to the child as to size and form; teach as well as be fun; help the child gain some competence for living in the world; strengthen good relationships with people; and arouse wonderment, imagination and creative thinking. Most of all, toys should help the child relive and clarify his experiences.[8] Toys should reinforce, not contradict, the positive values we are trying to instill in them.

It is important to remember that toys themselves are not the primary influence on a child's development. Instead, reasearch by child development specialists and psychologists has shown that the influence of toys on a child's development is secondary to the behavioral examples shown by parents and other adults. Experts encourage adults to take time out from their daily routines to play with their children, because adults are a child's best learning tool. A *USA Today* article featured a mother whom many child development experts would call a "playful parent." This mother, who lives in Atlanta, is willing to make a fool of herself to teach her child one of life's most important skills: how to play.

"I will romp and stomp, and just let it all go with my kids," she said to the *USA Today* reporters. *"I will slide in the mud, run under the backyard sprinkler, giggle till I cry.* It took me a while to learn to get down on my hands and knees so that I don't tower over them. I've discovered that you can learn a lot about each other and have fun when you're crawling around together." Brian Sutton-Smith, a professor of educa-

tion at University of Pennsylvania in Philadelphia, says children are not born knowing how to play. Children do not play by instinct; rather, they must learn to play from others, he told the newspaper.

Many adults neglect this responsibility because they are too busy with jobs and chores. As a result, television becomes a substitute for the parent, teaching children about everything from sex to God. These values, however, would be better taught by the parents themselves. Through heavy dosages of television, children begin to view what they see on TV as reality.

On the average, children between two and five years old watch more than 30 hours of TV each week, making it the dominant activity in the child's life. Television replaces essential play activities with nothing, with passivity rather than activity.[9] Children need to be stimulated in order to develop and learn. But, the passive nature of television tends to hypnotize the child, to blank out his connections with himself and the world. Television deprives the child of the opportunity to respond actively to an incoming stimulus. As a result, the child is subjected to a bombardment of sound and pictures at a pace he cannot control or alter. More importantly though, television robs the child of the hours needed for play, which is necessary for healthy development.[10]

To turn the passive influence of television into an active and learning experience for a child takes time and effort. Adults should use children's television viewing to initiate active play. Psychologists Dorothy and Jerome Singer, co-directors of the Yale University Family Television Research and Consultation Center, suggest encouraging children to make up games and skits based on television programs and put on their own shows by constructing the TV set out of a carton and using dolls or cardboard cutout figures as puppet players.[11] First, be sure the shows do not portray occult practices or violence. Otherwise, you will be reinforcing those ideals. The children should be encouraged to use their imagination during this creative play. Also, parents should try to elicit thoughtful responses from the child about shows they watch. This also will help turn a passive experience into an active one.[12]

Although some families may turn television into an active experience, it is generally true that *the more television a child watches, the greater the negative impact on his learning and development.* It is not only the quality of shows the child watches, but also the quantity that contributes to the negative impact.

In his studies a half-century ago, Jean Piaget, a pioneer in the studies of how children learn, observed that children learn through self-motivated, discovery play, inventing both the problems and the solutions according to an innate and universal "readiness" timetable.[13] Human beings are programmed to survive by discoveries made through trial and error. In a sense, when children play, they are carrying out the human "program for survival."

5

SYMBOLS OF THE REAL WORLD?

We all have had toys, even if we came from a poor family. In that case, we just had a fewer number of them. But it might come as a surprise to you that through the ages, toys were not always available. It was not until the last half of the eighteenth century that toys became industrialized. At this time, toy shows traveled around like circuses and toy shops were established in major cities.

At the time of the advent of toys, children in England were beginning to be regarded for the first time as consumers and agents for the ambition of middle class parents.[1] Children were being regarded as children, and not miniature adults. For the first time, books were being written specifically for children, using simple language and large print. Also, children were being dressed for the first time specifically in children's clothes. Children of middle class parents were being sent to elementary schools to learn the new commercial (boys) and social (girls) opportunities of the Industrial Revolution. Even some working class parents sought access to reading and schools for their children.[2]

As time passed, toys had a major influence on changes in the family structure. This is not to say that toys were necessarily a bad influence. In a sense, they became a "crutch" for parents.

Three hundred years ago, the family was the center of work, politics, religion, education and reproduction.[3] Today, however, most of these functions are attended to elsewhere—in factories, political parties, churches, schools and family planning centers. Modern society prizes individualistic ambition in business and school. According to Brian Sutton-Smith in an article, *Ambivalence in Toyland,* written in *Natural History,* "people are rewarded for putting aside their marriages, children, families, communities and churches in favor of the public worlds of work and success."[4] Toys are a bulwark against the many forces of modern society that threaten to tear families apart. Thus, parents often use toys to remind family members of the "togetherness" they wish to preserve.[5]

Herein lies a paradox. Although parents give toys to children to restore strained social bonds and to insure togetherness, the family rarely spends much time playing as a family. **The parent who gets down on the floor to play with a child on Christmas is doing something that will be seldom repeated throughout the rest of the year.** On the other hand, many parents believe one of the main purposes of toys is to insure that children can occupy themselves without demanding a great deal of the parents' time, while the parents pursue careers. Because of the times, toys have become a "crutch" that parents rely on heavily.

Modern society places heavy emphasis on solitary striving for achievement. Toys further this emphasis by training children's minds and habituating them to solitary, impersonal activity.[6] However, too much solitary play, as well as too much television, inhibits a child's ability to interact with others and develop into a well-rounded individual who is able to adjust to society. On the other hand, if a child never plays with toys, he will not be fully able to develop his imagination. Remember, imagination plays an important role in a child's development. Children should be given a balanced diet of solitary and social play.

Toys are the primary vehicle children use to display their imagination. When a child plays with a baby doll or truck, his imagination is free to determine the role that the toy will have. In this sense, the toy becomes an extension of the child's psyche.[7] *In a child's imagination, the personality assigned to a toy, either by himself or someone else, is often as real as his parents and peers.* The subjective nature of a toy is enhanced to unlimited proportions depending on the child's interest. Many researchers have claimed that toys are important aspects of the overall environment that shapes a child's moral and social ethics.[8]

With the influx of television in our lives, it often shapes the personalities that children give their toys. Today, many major toy companies simultaneously release toys and cartoons. As a result, when children watch cartoons, images are formed in their minds regarding how the toy should behave and the various "powers" it has. Then, the child re-enacts these behaviors when engaging in solitary play.

Some people believe this behavior is harmless. In truth, this re-enacting what has been shown on television inhibits the development of the child's imagination. *When a child watches a cartoon and then plays with a toy connected to that cartoon, he is no longer projecting himself into the toy.* Instead, cartoons have programmed the child to play with toys in a certain way. He has been told what character the action figure has, as well as the figure's abilities, personality and talents. The cartoons even have set the surrounding for the character. Through the influence of television, the child knows all these pieces of information about the toy when he picks it up.

For this reason, it is not healthy for children to play with toys linked to television shows. When a toy is linked to occult symbolisms, the negative influences are more severe.

When playing with a toy that has pre-programmed occult symbols, a child focuses his imagination on the occult. Even if a child does not have a toy that is associated with occult-oriented cartoons, he still may incorporate these occult images, which he has seen on cartoons, into his "let's pretend" world by pretending to be the character himself. This is a form of *visualization.*

Parents would be wise to be aware of the toys with which their children are playing, especially those containing occult symbols. Often, parents are too busy to actively monitor the child's toys. More often than not, though, parents do not realize the harmful effects toys can have on children. Most people view toys as cute and innocent, merely child's play. They consider toys to be harmless and nothing to be concerned about.

I am reminded of several instances when parents realized, unfortunately not until after some damage was done, of toys' effects on children. Some of these include:

A mother and her young son riding in the car were listening to a sermon on the radio. The minister started to pray, "Our Lord God, the master of the universe . . . ." The little boy jumped up from the back seat of the car and said, "Mommy, God isn't the master of the universe, *He-Man* is."

There was one little girl who ran around the house doing everything by the *power of Grayskull. Grayskull* is a demon-possessed castle in the *He-Man* series. But, after hearing me speak at a church, she started running around the house doing everything by the *power of Jesus.*

There is another case where a mother and her young son were in the car and they just had a near collision. Understandably, the mother was shaken. So, the little boy put his hand on his mother's lap and said, "Don't worry, Mommy, *He-Man* would have saved us."

Once my father was ministering at a church and he mentioned my ministry. Briefly he also mentioned *He-Man*. After the service, a little boy was seen in the parking lot running in circles while holding his *He-Man* figure in his hand. He kept repeating, "*He-Man* has more power than Jesus. *He-Man* has more power than Jesus."

Toys, especially those linked to cartoons, often present mystical characters capable of impossible feats. These toys and cartoons glamorize mystical "powers." Unfortunately, children believe these images. They begin to believe that these characters are real and more powerful than Jesus. Jesus did not constantly perform "mystical" deeds. In fact, Jesus' walk on earth was a very *real* one; He lived his life as any other human. On the other hand, *He-Man* lives a very *unreal* life. Because a child is exposed constantly to these images, it is no wonder he views *He-Man* as all-powerful. The workings of *subtle deception* already have taken place.

How can you tell which toys to stay away from? There are three categories of toys: occult, amoral and Christian. *Occult toys* are those that teach witchcraft, violence, sex and Humanism. Simply stated, Humanism is a religion which teaches that man is his own god and man is the measure of all things.[9] For *occult toys,* it is most important to consider the link between the toy and the cartoon. *Amoral toys* do not teach morality, neither good nor bad. *Amoral toys* include such things as baby dolls, trucks, cars and educational toys which teach the ABCs, numbers, etc. *Christian toys* are those which teach Christian principles and instill moral values in a child.

Problems arise for parents when they buy toys for their children, especially if the child is with them. Television has glorified many toys through cartoons and advertisements. Add a little peer pressure to that, and the child feels he "must" have the toy. This forces parents to make a decision which could anger the child.

Well-known columnist Leo Buscaglia has written a syndicated column about struggles in toy stores. While browsing through a toy store, he heard a struggle going on in another aisle between a mother and a son over the purchase of a *model battle station*. An excerpt of that column follows:[10]

> "Why would you want such a thing, Johnny?" she asked.
>
> "Oh, Mom. Look, it has a battering ram and special laser and rocket launchers."
>
> The mother sighed and looked toward the exit. But the hard sell was coming next.
>
> "You see it on TV, Mom. It's the greatest. Besides, Joey's mom is getting him one. Pleeeeease, Mom."
>
> The magical appeal of television and a little peer pressure made the struggle brief. Johnny would soon be doing battle with Joey.
>
> Perhaps the mother wanted to hold out for something more instructive. Perhaps there was even a hint of moral objection in her resistance to a toy, which, like so many others, simulates violence. As I perused the shelves, I couldn't help but notice how many toys are oriented toward war and combat.
>
> Instead of the toy guns and rubber knives I remember as a child, kids today can wage interplanetary war in their backyards.

A vast majority of toys on the market today deal with violence and the occult. Even *G.I. Joe,* a toy that has been on the market for the last 30 years, has changed with the times. Today, *G.I. Joe* is "outfitted for the '80s with *assault copters, jet skystrikers, armored missile vehicles* and *twin laser blasters.*"[11] With the assistance of television shows like *He-Man* and movies, such as *Rambo* and *Conan the Barbarian,* war-like toys are gaining popularity among children. Although many parents express concern over these toys and the *barbarization* effects that they have on children, the toy industry has not suffered. In fact, the toy industry is booming, with no signs of a reversal in that trend. But, the types of toys are not the only changes that have occurred in the toy industry.

The toy industry itself has changed dramatically in the last 20 years. Twenty years ago, if a toy firm did $10-$20 million in sales, it was considered large. Then, new marketing tactics were tried: big advertisement blitzes, especially during prime children's viewing times, and simultaneously releasing toys and cartoons. The tactics worked. More toys are being bought than ever before. Not too long ago, Mattel was doing a $10-$20 million business a year. In 1985, the figures jumped to $1 billion a year; *He-Man and Masters of the Universe* accounted for more than one-half of Mattel's sales. The toy industry expects to reach $16 billion in the near future. Toys R Us, known as TOY on the New York Stock Exchange, is a leader in the retailing business of toys.[12] The firm expects an annual growth rate of more than 25 percent over the next five years. In fact, TOY accounts for about 12-14 percent of all toy sales in the U.S.[13] According to *The Hume Moneyletter*, 60 percent of all toy purchases are made during the eight weeks preceding Christmas.[14] The report further explains that the recent boom in the toy industry is the biggest since World War II.

Researchers offer many explanations for the sharp rise in toy sales. Some say the increase is a result of the "echo baby boom." The "Baby Boomers" of the 1950s and '60s have reached child-bearing years and are creating an "echo baby boom." Thus, if more children are being born, more toys will be bought.[15] Others say it is because more families are headed by two-career parents. These say, as a result of the two careers, there will be an increase of income, thus allowing more to be spent on toys, and **parents will buy the toys to promote "solitary activity" for the child so that he will be "occupied" while the parents are busy.**[16] Whatever the reason, it cannot be ignored that toy sales are booming. And with each toy sold, especially those promoting the occult and violence, our youths are being exposed to negative and harmful influences.

With the increasing need for "good" toys, parents are reminded that there are several toy companies specializing in *Christian toys*. However, these toys are not as widely distributed as toys from other firms because they have not been in business as long as Mattel, Hasbro and others.

6

THE ELECTRONIC PARENT

Did you know?

Preschoolers spend more time watching TV than it takes to earn a college degree.

By the time of high school graduation, most children will have spent only 11,000 hours in school, but more than 15,000 hours in front of the television.

Only about one-third of all parents attempt to control the amount and content of television their children watch.

Television has the power to enhance or stunt a child's growth.[1]

No matter how startling, these facts are true. As a matter of fact, children are actually spending more time today in front of the television set than the reported 15,000 hours. The 1978 study that reported those findings was repeated in 1984. The new findings indicate that children are now spending an average of 22,000 hours in front of the television. This is twice the amount of time that the child is actually in school. Also, these findings represent an increase in viewing time of more than 1,000 hours a year.

Although television is just a little more than thirty years old, it has profoundly changed the way we think, live and raise our children. In fact, it has probably changed our lives more than any other invention of the modern world. What other inanimate object would a parent entrust to their child's care? Probably nothing, other than the TV. Many times, television serves as a babysitter for children while a parent is busy in another part of the house. But more and more, with an increasing number of mothers in the work force, children are coming home to an empty house with verbal instructions from their parents to do their homework and watch TV until the parents get home from work.

Next to parents, television is the most important teacher that a child has, if for no other reason than because of the massive amount of time that children spend in front of the television set. As a matter of fact, sleeping is the only activity that children engage in more than watching television. And, it is important to remember that what a child learns from this *electronic parent* can either interfere with or enhance his growth.[2]

Most psychologists believe that 80 percent of a child's character and personality is developed by the time he is five years old. Also, it has been reported that humans learn 80 percent of all they will learn during the first five years of life. These are the impressionable years. In fact, these years have been described by researchers as the "habit-training and character building" phase of a child's life. Basic attitudes and character traits are learned through specific experiences in a child's life.[3] Various studies have reported that, at any time of the day or night, preschoolers make up 22 percent of the viewing audience. In fact, preschoolers watch between 22 and 26 hours of television each week. If a child is spending more time watching television than any other activity, the ideas he picks up from the shows will have a definite impact on his values and how he views the world. During these formative years, it is important that a child spend more time with his parents and engaging in social and imaginative play, rather than watching television.

Another corresponding study also produced astonishing results. A group of preschoolers were fitted with hidden microphones to wear while at home. After reviewing the tapes, researchers found that the average American father spends only 37 seconds a day in direct communication with his preschool child. This is far less than the amount of time that the same child watches television each day. Therefore, it is no wonder child development experts are calling television the *electronic parent*; in many households, television has usurped the role once held by parents.

Many parents have often remarked that watching television is the only activity in which their child will sit still for hours without complaining. Scientifically, that does not seem so unusual. Marie Winn, in her book, *The Plug-In Drug*,[4] describes this same behavior. The type of show one is watching does not seem to matter; the brain reacts the same to all television shows. When children, as well as adults, watch television, electrodes in the brain release a slight depressant. As a result, the body reacts to the TV much in the same manner as to a physically addictive, minor depressant drug.[5] Children then become "glued" to the television, watching it for three or four hours without taking a bathroom break.

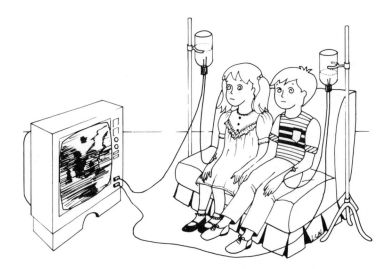

According to Winn, the most insidious aspect of this "drug" is "that it is given by the parent to the child, not for the child's benefit, but in order for the parent to have some peace and quiet."[6] In Winn's view, sitting the child in front of the television set is not unlike administering some lethargy-inducing drug to the child and then sitting him down in the nearest corner to stare at the wall. But, staring at a wall will not affect a child's attitudes. Whereas, while watching television, the child's attitudes toward life, other people and the world are being formed in ways that many parents do not agree with at all.[7]

As children watch television in this affixed state, they begin to receive information on a passive level, rather than actively deciphering the information as it is received. While a child passively receives incoming stimuli, the right hemisphere of the brain is developed, but the development of the left hemisphere of the brain is inhibited.[8] The right hemisphere controls visual-spatial development in a child; the left hemisphere controls verbal-analytic development. Thus, prolonged television watching can stunt a child's development of analytic skills, hindering his abilities to learn on his own.[9] As a result, he leaves his mind open for the influence of *subtle deception*.

It is important to remember that the effects of *subtle deception* are not readily noticed. Instead, *subtle deception* affects the child a little at a time over the years. The effects of *subtle deception* can be likened to the ocean's tide. Each time the tide flows into shore, it brings a little sediment from the ocean's floor and washes it onto the beach. At first, passers-by may not notice the sediment. But over time, if the beaches are not cleaned up, the litter will keep building up until the sand is covered with seaweed and other sediment.

A child's mind works in much the same way. You will recall that a youngster's mind is like a sponge, soaking up anything and everything he encounters. These images, absorbed by a child's mind, then become the building blocks that he uses for making sense out of life and the world.[10] In *The Gift of Play,* Maria Piers and Genevieve Landau say that the oft-repeated truism, "It's not the quantity, but the quality that counts," should be turned around when dealing with the amount of time that children spend watching television.[11] Although "good" shows are much better for children than "poor" ones, the more television a child watches, the worse the effect. Prolonged television-watching, regardless of what they are watching, does in fact imperil young children.[12] In a recent *USA Today* article, it was reported that most child experts say that preschoolers should watch a maximum of one hour of television a day. The experts then added that two hours a day was acceptable for older children.[13]

To grow and develop, both mentally and physically, children need to use their imagination and mind to make sense of the world around them. Television, however, does not allow a child to discover or learn on his own. Instead, it continually feeds the child's mind with images and values at a pace the child cannot control. Therefore, the child is then bombarded with incoming information without any opportunity to make his own mental images.[14] He learns to accept what he sees as true, without actively trying to figure out why it is true.

No matter what the show is, whether "educational" or not, the child is learning. Researchers have found that shows do not have to be "educational" to teach. In fact, many child development experts believe that shows designed to teach reading and math skills are more harmful than many "conventional" programs. These "educational" shows prevent the child from exercising his own mind and imagination, which is necessary for the child's healthy growth.[15]

"Educational" television, the shows most endorsed by parents, have many flaws of which parents should be aware.

Most parents praise "educational" shows because they believe the shows are teaching the child basic skills. But, researchers are finding that these shows do not present the material in a manner that would be conducive to the child's learning. Child development experts claim it is undesirable to impose adult-structured game-lessons on preschoolers.[16] Also, these shows tend to present the material at a frantic pace. The child should be given time and the opportunity to respond to what he sees with his own feelings and thoughts. A preschooler is just beginning to conceptualize and to understand and control his feelings and behavior. He needs time and the freedom to practice thinking and ways of behaving on his own. However, "educational" shows tend to present the material in a barrage of brightly colored images, zooming off and on the screen to the accompaniment of loud rock music. As a result, this bombardment of the child's senses does not give him the opportunity to respond with his own thoughts and feelings.[17]

Parents often question if reading to a child will have the same negative impact on his creativity and learning abilities that watching television does. But, the impact is not the same. In fact, most child development experts encourage parents to read to their children. In their book, *The Gift of Play,* Piers and Landau describe why reading to a child is beneficial:[18]

> In being read to or told a story, a child has to make up his own images about the people, events, scenes in the story. He brings them to life in his imagination. Moreover, he has considerable control over the pace and rhythm of the material presented. Children often ask an adult who is reading to them to go back and read something over, or to stop and talk about what is happening on the page. None of this is possible in watching television. The story rushes on, the prefabricated images flash on and off.

Although television can be a "window to the world,"[19]

broadening a child's knowledge and interests, it also can introduce a child to negative situations which they may never see or experience in real life. The effect television will have on the child depends largely on how you, as the parent, guide television viewing in the home.[20]

Too often, children are left to watch television on their own without much parental guidance. This is where many problems arise. Many times, what they see on television conflicts with what they see in their own lives. When they receive these conflicting messages, they get confused. Unless an adult is there to explain what the child has seen, the child often will believe what he sees on television as real.

Until a child is seven years old, he sees television as reality. He has no concept of fantasy and reality. He views everything in a very literal sense. For example, have you ever tried to tell a three-year-old, "We'll do it tomorrow"? He will probably be back in an hour or so asking if it is tomorrow yet. The same is true with television. No matter how much we try to explain to a child that what he sees on television is fantasy and not reality, it is beyond the child's developmental capabilities to comprehend such information. In turn, the child may "parrot" the explanation given him, in order to avoid discipline. According to Cheryl A. Cotthelf, head of *The Children's Advertising and Commercial Review,* "children undergo qualitative changes in the way they organize and use information. The development moves from a literal acceptance of what they perceive as reality to a more sophisticated level of being able to make inferences and eventually judgments." Until a child can perceive the difference between television and reality, it is important to monitor what he watches and to discuss the shows with the child after they are over.

To give an example from my own experience. When I was two years old, I watched an episode of *Lassie.* At the end of the episode, Lassie ran into a burning barn. Then the show ended with "to be continued." In my mind, Lassie was gone; she was dead. I was upset. I remember crying because I thought Lassie had burned to death and that she would have to be replaced. While I cried, my father tried to tell me that it was just a television show and that it was not real. He told me that Lassie would be all right. But I still did not believe him. My dad then, in desperation, faked a call to the program producers to make sure that Lassie was OK. Only after my dad hung up the phone did I believe that Lassie was really OK. Years later, however, I learned that my dad had faked that phone call. You see, as a child, I believed what I saw on television. In my mind, what I saw on TV was real.

Television does not present a "real" picture of the world. In fact, much of what is shown on television is in direct conflict with the values we try to instill in our children. As an example, less than five percent of all sexual scenes shown on television are scenes between married couples. That means that 95 percent of all sexual scenes presented are comprised of adultery, homosexuality, fornication, etc. Is this what we want our children to believe as reality? This is what our children are being programmed to believe.

Still, the unrealistic nature of television does not seem to concern many parents. Many argue that they watched a lot of television as a child and they were not "affected." But, who can say that they were not affected. Anyone who grew up watching television, and yet says he was not affected by it is only kidding himself. It is important to remember that television fare has changed dramatically in the last 20 years. Today's television shows are saturating our children with violence and occultism. They are desensitizing our children to accept violence as part of life and that it is nothing to be shocked about.[21] There are also many parents who allow their children to watch violent and occult shows because they want their children to experience "reality," and do not want to deprive their children of the same experiences and material goods their friends have. Parents believing this are jeopardizing their children's souls by exposing them to evil.[22] In his *Media Spotlight* article, Albert Dager contends that there are enough evil influences in the world that the children must contend with without parents providing them opportunities to pervert their imaginations.[23]

A task force of *The American Academy of Pediatrics* did a 16-month study on children and television. Some of their findings were reported in a recent *USA Today* article:

> Repeated exposure to television violence can make children both violent and accepting of real-life violence. Another study has found that by the time a child graduates from high school, he will have seen 18,000 killings on television.
>
> Television watching promotes obesity. Children eat high-calorie junk foods because of the many junk-food commercials and because TV-watching has become a traditional snack time for children.
>
> Television encourages the use of drugs, alcohol and tobacco by glamorizing them. The heroes whom children emulate are often shown smoking and drinking beer.
>
> Television's unrealistic sexual relationships may contribute to the risk of teen pregnancy. On television, relationships develop rapidly and the risk of pregnancy is rarely considered.

Christian parents, especially, are concerned about the effects of television on their children. Christians are generally not represented in television in a real manner. Christians generally are not depicted on television as intelligent. In fact, by excluding an accurate representation of Christians, television is not very representative of the vast majority of people in the world.

Television generally does not give much credence to Christian beliefs or concepts. As you know, television gives credence to the occult and psychic power by presenting it and not trying to disprove it. Many shows, especially cartoons, are "saturated" with the occult. Children see the occult as being "all-powerful" and real. Thus, because most characters use the occult to get out of difficult situations, children see this as a real solution.

"Layer upon layer," these images have a negative influence on a child. A little at a time, these images begin to surface in the child's mind, and he expects real life to be like that on television. One teacher remarked concern that the "children in her class were used to seeing all problems, no matter how complex, solved within an hour on television. And if it was not solved, the problem would be over in an hour anyway."[24] This often causes frustration for a child.

Researchers and members of the task force from *The American Academy of Pediatrics* have developed some guidelines for parents to follow so that television viewing will benefit the child and have a minimal amount of negative influence:

(1) Limit children's viewing time. Plan and monitor what they watch. Experts also encourage parents to monitor their own television viewing so as to set an example for the children.

(2) Never use television as a reward or punishment. This makes it seem more important to the child.

(3) Discuss television violence after seeing it in a program. Talk about the difference between real life and television make-believe.

Perhaps, if parents take a more active role in the child's television viewing, the child will not be deceived into believing that what he sees on TV is real. Over time, the negative influences of *subtle deception* may then begin to fade. Otherwise, the *subtle deception* of television will begin eroding the Christian values that parents try to teach their children.

7

COMMERCIALTOONS

For years, manufacturers have based products on popular television characters and shows. Today, however, the process is different. Cartoon writers and toy designers now collaborate efforts to release toys and cartoons simultaneously. In fact, almost every cartoon released today is connected with a toy; thus, the cartoons and toys promote each other. This causes confusion: Are the cartoons commercials? or Are the commercials cartoons?

The use of product-based programs indicates how little care and creativity go into children's programming on commercial television. However, Action for Children's Television, otherwise known as ACT, monitors children's programming to ensure that children are not being exploited by the manufacturers. On Oct. 11, 1983, ACT filed a complaint with the Federal Communications Commission claiming that a number of children's programs are nothing more than 30-minute commercials for products. Peggy Charren, president of ACT, has been quoted as saying, "These 30-minute commercials take advantage of children who may not be able to tell the difference between a show and an advertisement. Children don't understand what a vested interest is."

Frank Orme, head of the non-profit National Association for Better Broadcasting, also objects to cartoons that are based on trademarked products. An example of this is *He-Man and Masters of the Universe,* which is based on the action-figure series. Both the figures and title of the show are trademarked. "It's an exploitation of kids—the entire program becomes a commercial," he said.

To understand the effect *commercialtoons* have on children, we must first understand how a child views and perceives television and commercials. As I said in an earlier chapter, children do not view television the same way adults do; their perceptions are different. As children grow older, they learn to process the information they receive differently and then make inferences and judgments on what they have seen.

Because a child under seven years old cannot distinguish between fantasy and reality, he is not able to distinguish between commercials and regular television shows. This has become especially difficult since commercial writers use animation to sell products. When an animated commercial is sandwiched between an animated cartoon, it is even more difficult for children to tell the difference. Animation, however, is not the only problem of commercials. The primary problem is that *children view commercials as "public service announcements."* They think they should have these advertised products. Also, commercials often instill peer pressure by saying such things as "Be sure to have your mom get this so you will be the first kid on the block to have (such and such)." Consider this familiar scene:

> A mother pushes a cart down the cereal aisle at the grocery store. She reaches for a box of *Captain Crunch*, knowing full well that the cereal she is about to buy is 50 to 75 percent sugar. Shortly after feeding it to little Joey and Suzy, she knows they will be "bouncing off the walls."
>
> So, why does she do it? She buys the cereal because little Joey and Suzy spend every Saturday morning "glued" to the television. Between each scene of their favorite cartoons are animated *Captain Crunch* commercials. During the commercials, *Captain Crunch* says he has the "best-tasting cereal around." *Captain Crunch* also offers a "secret spy decoder ring"

to decode the secret spy message on the back of the box.

Now the advertisers have created an advocate in the home, and for about the 400th time little Joey and Suzy say, in their most whiny voice, "I want *Captain Crunch*." And again, Mom gives in.

It is this type of influence that has ACT concerned. Commercials push toys, cereals, sweets and even vitamins. Many pharmaceutical companies have manufactured vitamins that are linked to popular television shows. Some of these are *Bugs Bunny, Flintstones* and *Cabbage Patch Kids Chewable Vitamins*. In the February 1986 issue of *Toy and Hobby World*,[1] it was reported that ACT has filed a complaint with the Federal Trade Commission against Pharmed Laboratories. ACT wants to prevent the vitamin manufacturer from promoting its *Cabbage Patch Kids Chewable Vitamins* during television shows with a significant audience of young people. The complaint follows the airing of the commercials during Saturday morning children's programs.

In the complaint, ACT cites a 1976 Federal Trade Commission consent order that concluded "such (vitamin) advertising can induce children to take excessive amounts of vitamins, which can be dangerous to their health." ACT says *Cabbage Patch* vitamins are promoted to appear like toys and candy. As proof of their claim, the group cites a scene in the 30-second commercial in which a young boy claims, "They're shaped like little cabbage buds," and a little girl says, "Cherry and berry's my favorite."[2]

Although parents may not realize how their children view television and commercials, advertisers do. Advertisers know children accept what they see on television as reality; therefore, they are focusing more on intercutting animation and reality portions of the commercial. However, this causes many problems:

(1) This may create an illusion about a product's performance that can exceed its actual capabilities.

(2) It may interfere with a child's ability to access the product by reducing the already brief amount of time the actual product is seen in a realistic place setting—a place setting that the child will experience.

(3) It has the potential to leave the child with a somewhat distorted image of what the actual product will be like when he gets it.

In an article in the *The Detroit News*,[3] spokesmen for major toy companies agreed that cartoons based on their popular toy lines were basically designed to "create an awareness" for the toys. They also agreed that the shows helped support and improve the overall marketing of the products. Still, many claimed that selling toys was not the only reason for the shows. They insist the cartoons have merits of their own.

In the past, the "Big Three" networks—ABC-TV, CBS-TV and NBC-TV—steered away from programs created by toy companies.[4] But for the last two or three years, these networks also have aired shows that are directly linked with toys. There also have been some "Big Three" network shows that have had "spin-off" products.

Some people claim that cartoons may be too persuasive, planting psychological images that lead to preoccupation with cartoon characters and their toy replicas. This is especially true with younger children who are not able to deal with the "hard-sell" that takes place in many programs. Bruce Watkins, assistant professor of the Communications Department at the University of Michigan, told *The Detroit News* that children under seven years old are even more influenced by these types of shows. "One element of these shows that is really unfortunate is that they were created to sell toys as opposed to entertain children," he told the reporter.[5] In 1984, Watkins spent a year working with a

U.S. congressional subcommittee on telecommunications, consumer protection and finance.

Whatever the influence, toy companies are making money with these shows. In 1984, sales of *He-Man and Masters of the Universe* toys and paraphernalia topped $1 billion for Mattel. *He-Man,* which is Mattel's most popular toy line, also has been rated the top-rated independent children's show. After just one season, *Voltron, Defender of the Universe,* manufactured by Matchbox, was rated nationally as the second-highest weekday animated television show.

Nevertheless, toy companies are not relying on cartoons to make their money. They also are paying large sums of money to advertise their products. In the last quarter of 1985 alone, Mattel spent $40 million on advertising.[6] Although annual advertising expenditures by major toy and sporting goods manufacturers have been rising steadily, there was a significant increase in 1984. According to the *Television Bureau of Advertising Inc.,* companies spent an annual total of $305,980,400 in 1984; whereas, in 1983, the companies spent $213,802,800.[7]

With this amount of advertising in addition to the cartoons themselves, it is no wonder that the media are flooded with commercialtoons. But, companies do not stop with commercials and cartoons. Many, including *Rainbow Brite* and *Rock Lords,* also are licensing out the rights for film companies to make full-length feature movies based on the toy series. Another example of this is the 90-minute *Care Bear Movie,* which was basically a commercial for the new *Care Bear Cousins.* Realizing the effects that such a movie would have on sales, retailers ordered a half million of the toys to correspond with the introduction of the movie.[8] An example of this process, but in reverse, is the *Rubics Cube.* A few years ago, the *Rubics Cube* was a popular toy among the young and old. Soon thereafter, ABC introduced a cartoon based on the *Cube.*

Other popular commercialtoons today include: *Dungeons and Dragons, He-Man and Masters of the Universe, Smurfs, Shirttales* and *Transformers*. Commercialtoons do not just promote toys. Those promoting video games are also popular: *Saturday Supercade*, which stars *Donkey Kong, Donkey Kong Jr.* and *Uncle Pitfall*, and *Pac Man*.

Although commercialtoons linked to video games are popular, those promoting toys are still in the lead. Companies maintain children's interests by constantly releasing new episodes and new toys to correspond with those episodes. In September 1985, Hasbro released 65 new episodes of *Transformers*. In addition, Hasbro is spending $15 million in advertising for this series, and there are 35 companies producing *Transformers* products, such as party favors, sheets, etc. Mattel, in collaboration with Filmation Studios, creators of the animated *He-Man and Masters of the Universe* series, released 33 new episodes. To launch the new series, Filmation also produced a feature-length animated movie on *He-Man and Masters of the Universe*. The movie premiered in theaters in 10 major U.S. cities: Houston; Dallas; Washington, D.C.; New York; Los Angeles; Detroit; St. Louis; Chicago; Philadelphia and Boston. Press kits and collectors' posters were used to increase awareness of the new *He-Man* series.

The idea of connecting toys with cartoons was born in the fall of 1983 with the debut of *He-Man and Masters of the Universe.*[9] According to syndication experts, *He-Man* has been the single major factor in the new-production kid-syndicated activity. The *He-Man* strip also has renewed station and advertiser support. As a result, "kid stuff" has become the "right stuff."[10] Spurred by the ratings success of *He-Man and Masters of the Universe*, there has been a rise in new independent television stations, as well as a return of major children's advertisers with new brands, and in merchandising ties. As a result, "syndicated kid television" has come of age.[11]

Before the *He-Man* series, most shows offered during the afterschool hours were re-runs that had been re-running for the past several years. According to the president of World Events Productions, "*He-Man* 'broke the mold' for new cartoons coming into the TV syndication picture."[12] The senior vice president of Worldvision Enterprises agreed. "*He-Man* definitely has been a factor in the kid boom in that it represents the first time in a long while that a kid barter show has worked as a strip," he said.[13]

Since the debut of *He-Man and Masters of the Universe*, all major toy companies have followed the pattern. As a result, toy companies are surpassing all previous sales records and children's programming is booming. Because the shows were designed specifically for children does not necessarily mean they are "good." It does not mean they are filled with harmless and "cute" ideas.

In fact, most cartoons are far from being "cute." Many are extremely violent. The *He-Man* series averages 37 violent acts every half-hour; *Advanced Dungeons and Dragons*, 67; and *G.I. Joe* is one of the most violent cartoons, with 80 acts of violence evey half-hour.

After watching these, many children experience nightmares. In a letter, one father told me he had barred his children from watching *Scooby Doo* because it was causing his son to have nightmares. Other children become overly aggressive and hostile in their play after viewing violent shows. This same father said his sons constantly were fighting with their friends and each other. Finally, the father also barred *He-Man* cartoons. Although his children protested mildly, the father said the level of hostility decreased after a few days and the children began to *play* again, instead of waiting for the show to come on television.

Nevertheless, violence is not the only negative factor with cartoons. There also has been a significant increase in the amount of sexual innuendoes and occult symbolisms used. In most cartoons, the sexual overtones are subtle. Most women in cartoons are perfectly formed and wear skimpy clothing. Although this may seem extremely minor, it does leave open the opportunity for sexual fantasies. Besides, most women in the world are not perfectly formed. These images lead young boys to expect that their girlfriends will be beautiful and "perfect," and it can cause "unreal beauty expectations" in little girls.

Besides the skimpy clothes, sexual overtones are portrayed in other ways. *Robotech,* a cartoon series with 168 episodes, is considered to be highly sexual. The producer of the series has said, "It is not a robot show. Rather it is a science fiction adventure series and will have the dramatic sub-structure of a soap opera." The series has many of the same plots, as well as the male/female interactions, of any soap opera.

Occult symbolisms in cartoons are extremely prevalent. Many of the characters' names are linked to the occult; there is a significant amount of witchcraft, magic, sorcery and other occult practices being performed; and many of the objects used by the characters, such as a breastplate or staff, have occult symbols on them. But, the use of occult symbolisms does not end here. In fact, many of the messages spoken on the shows have their origins in Humanism and Eastern religions, such as *Hinduism* and *Buddhism.* There are thousands of examples of each of these, which can be gathered from watching any of the shows.

Many examples of the occult found in cartoons will be discussed here. It is important parents realize that most of these cartoons are associated with toys. If the shows have occult ideas, it is logical to assume that the toys also will have occult symbolisms. Many of the toys come with little comic books which are laden with the occult. Children are being bombarded with these ideas. First they see it on television; then they read the comics; and then they play with the toy, re-enacting some of the scenes they have seen or read; and lastly, they apply these concepts to other forms of play—such as when they and their friends are playing "let's pretend" without using any toys. At this time, the child himself assumes the role of a cartoon character, such as *He-Man,* rather than having a doll do the actions. This causes the ideas to become ingrained in the child's mind.

BLACK STAR

To give an example of the blatant use of the occult in these toys which are linked to cartoons, let us consider *Black Star.* Every figure in the *Black Star* series comes with its own *glow-in-the-dark alien demon.* I am not inferring that these demonic-looking creatures are in fact demons. In truth, that is the exact description written on the outside of the package in which the figures come. Some of the action figures in the series are *Overlord,* the invincible wizard, and *Karday,* the wizard king. Like the other *Black Star* figures, *Overlord* and *Karday* come with a *glow-in-the-dark alien demon.*

Manufacturers have determined that a child will own approximately $72 worth of toys from any particular series. Therefore, if a child owns $72 worth of toys from *Black Star,* he would have six to twelve *glow-in-the-dark alien demons* in his room. Are these the types of toys we want our children to play with? What types of dreams do you think these demons will cause a child to have?

ADVANCED DUNGEONS AND DRAGONS

This cartoon series is based on the occult game *Dungeons and Dragons.* This fantasy role-playing game involves characters who use magic and sorcery to obtain treasures. The cartoon series, like the game, emphasizes white and black witchcraft. This cartoon averages 67 acts of violence every half-hour. There is another chapter in this book devoted solely to the *Dungeons and Dragons* game.

HE-MAN and MASTERS OF THE UNIVERSE

Despite the unprecedented popularity of this cartoon series among children, many parents and adults have voiced great concerns about it. The entire series is based on occult practices: magic, sorcery, witchcraft, necromancy, etc. The show also blasphemes God by placing a mortal on the same plane as He. *He-Man* is known as the most powerful man in the universe—he is called *Master of the Universe*. How is this possible when God tells us that He alone is Master of the Universe? In another chapter of this book, I deal specifically with the occult images found in this series, as well as the *She-Ra, Princess of Power* series.

SMURFS

The *Smurfs* cartoon originated in Europe but has had unprecented success in the United States. It has been enthusiastically embraced by both children and parents. Everyone thinks the cartoon is "cute." But don't let that innocent facade fool you. Underneath the "cuteness" is a cartoon laden with the occult, which is presented mostly in the form of magic. This cartoon will be discussed in detail in the *Cute and Innocent?* chapter.

CARE BEARS

The occult images found in the *Care Bear* series are extremely subtle. On the surface, the *Care Bears* teach the children to express their feelings, especially those of love, to others. At first, these sound like very good ideas, but, they are Humanistic principles, which are in contradiction to God's teachings. Magic and Eastern religious ideals also are prevalent in this series. Because of the innocent appearance of the *Care Bear* series, I will discuss it more fully in the chapter on cute and innocent toys.

TRANSFORMERS

Some of the toys within the *Transformers* category, which include *Voltron, Robotech, GoBots* and *Transformers*, could be considered amoral, neither good nor bad. Others are so blatantly violent that they disturb many parents. Although the toys themselves are hard to categorize, we must look at the corresponding cartoons.

Most of the transformer-based cartoons are extremely violent. Others, such as *Voltron*, have heavy inferences to the occult. While still others, such as *Robotech*, are filled with sexual innuendoes. It is important that parents watch these series and decide which ones will be acceptable for the children to watch.

There are many other cartoons that are filled with violence and the occult. Among these are *The Thirteen Ghosts of Scooby Doo, Speed Racer, Tarzan, Spider Man* and *G.I. Joe*. All of these should be considered unsuitable for children of any age.

Another fact to consider about cartoons in general is pointed out by Chuck Jones, creator of *Pepe Le Pew* and the *Roadrunner and Coyote*.[14] Jones said that the implication in cartoons is that "if you are ugly then you are evil, and if you are cute or pretty then you are OK." It is horrifying to think that children could grow up with this thinking. If they did, how would they handle those with physical handicaps? Would they think that these people are evil?

As in all television shows, there is always the risk that children will imitate dangerous acts that have been performed on television. There have been many cases where children have died while trying to "fly out the window" while imitating *Superman*. There is another case involving a child's death in which the parents were awarded an undisclosed sum of money. In this case, a six-year-old

Michigan boy died after copying a hanging scene, detail for detail, that was portrayed on a Saturday morning *Scooby Doo* cartoon.[15]

If all the occult and violent acts were not enough, consider the following radio broadcast that was featured in the *Moral Majority Report:*[16]

If you have been listening to this commentary over the last five years, then you know that I have touched on almost every subject imaginable that is of interest to those of us who are conservatives. You may say, there's nothing new he could talk about. There isn't an outrage I haven't heard. Well listen to this and see if this doesn't top the list.

The Los Angeles-based Alliance for Gay and Lesbian Artists in the Entertainment Industry has called on those who make the Saturday morning cartoons, which our children watch, to begin depicting homosexual couples in cartoons.

According to a report in *Electronic Media* magazine, Charles Uszler, a spokesman for the Alliance, says he is not calling for homosexuals to be in the forefront of the cartoons, nor is he calling for discussions of their sexuality. He thinks, though, that children need to know that same-sex couples exist and can live together in a domestic environment.

With the homosexuals already represented on television, certainly a lot more than, say, Christians and Jews, the battle for gay legitimacy now may be extending to our children via the Saturday morning cartoons.

If I did not need a television set for the news and public affairs I must watch as a journalist, I would seriously consider getting rid of the box altogether. I already control my children's access to it and want to know the content of a show before they watch it.

I take the trash out twice a week to be collected by the garbage man. But with television, it is increasingly a case of bringing the trash into the house seven days and nights a week. It has so much garbage on it that it might violate clean air standards of the Environmental Protection Agency.

There have been numerous stories of families who have tried doing without television for varying periods of time. I have never read a report that shows they regretted their decision. After an initial withdrawal period, most of them report improved communication, improved grades and improved reading skills.

It won't be much longer, given the current trend, when television is as constantly dirty as a sewer or septic tank. You wouldn't want your children playing in those places either, would you?

I'm Cal Thomas.

Cartoons, although they are animated children's shows, should not be taken lightly. Some of these shows are as heavily occult as an actual book of witchcraft; others are as sexual as a soap opera; and still others are as violent as a "Rated R" movie. Children should not be subjected to these images. They can cause nightmares and exaggerated aggressiveness. Yes, these shows were designed specifically for children, but they are unsuitable for children.

8

CUTE AND INNOCENT?

"Ooooh they're cute; they're fuzzy and cuddly! They're soft and so inviting of hugs and love." What are they? TOYS! Have you ever walked by a toy store and, despite the worries on your mind, your eyes were attracted to the display? It's no wonder. Toy stores are so inviting; they are even visually exciting. The array of colors capture the attention, causing even adults to reminisce about their own childhood toys.

They are pink. Some are blue. And others are purple. They have rainbow hair. They look like Raggedy Ann dolls. They are soft and cuddly. They are fuzzy and cute, but not necessarily "innocent." Many of these toys, even the ones that tug on our heartstrings as being so adorable, portray occult symbolisms.

My purpose for writing this book is not to condemn parents for permitting their children to play with certain toys, but to make them aware of these *subtle influences*. Unless one is made aware of these dangers, toys seem harmless. Once "enlightened," it is easy to see the negative influences these toys have on children. Innocent minds are filled with images laden with the occult. Through these "cute and innocent" toys, a wedge is inserted to make a wider gap for Satan and his influences to enter a child's mind, thereby, leaving him susceptible to incorporate these negative influences into his daily experience.

Again, these changes do not happen overnight. It takes years of having the mind saturated with images directed by Satan as he tries to stimulate the mind to focus on vain or carnal fantasies. Various means, such as television, movies, music, pornography, books and magazines, peer pressure and toys, are used to accomplish this end. Although some toys are blatantly occult, they are not the only ones which warrant our concern. To the contrary! It is the "cute and innocent" toys, filling our children with subliminal images, with which we must be concerned.

Often, knowledgeable parents will prohibit their children from playing with certain toys which are outright occult or violent. After doing so, these parents feel safe that their children are receiving "images" which have Christian values. But, if a child continues to play with certain "cute and innocent" toys that may portray occult images, his mind still will be corrupted, albeit in a "quiet" way, leaving the parent to wonder "how." A child's mind soaks up "all" images, whether consciously or not.[1] In time, these unconscious images will have as negative an effect as those which were presented in a blatant manner.

As the word "occult" implies, many of the symbolisms are hidden, concealed, visible only to the knowledgeable eye. I am not advocating that a person should burn their "cute and innocent" toys. I **am** suggesting, however, that before buying a toy, study it. Then, decide if that toy's symbols are in line with Scripture.

In many instances, there really is no problem with the toy itself. *The real danger lies in the occult and violent images connected with the toy which are conveyed to the child via cartoons, television and movies.* As a child watches these shows, he sees the producer's idea of the toy's capabilities. He watches the toy as it displays certain "powers" and projects certain images through the cartoon or movie. Then, when the child plays with that toy, he visualizes the toy with the pre-programmed "powers" and characteristics; thus, if the toy displays certain occult characteristics, occult images are being programmed into his mind. It is far better for a child to use his God-given imagination to bring life to a toy, than to have the toy manufacturer determine that toy's characteristics. As we discuss some of the "cute and innocent" toys, I will be more specific about those which have been negatively influenced by television or films.

Often, I am asked, "Why are so many toys and cartoons today based on occult symbolisms?" Parents often remark how toys have changed over the years, from the ones that they played with as a child to those available for today's children. For instance, years ago *G.I. Joe* was just an "army" doll for little boys. Today, however, the *G.I. Joes* on the toy shelves are much more combat-oriented. There is even a *G.I. Joe pocket-patrol pack,* which is a packet of portable miniature soldiers that can be carried on the belt for "combat on the go."[2] Although *G.I. Joe* may have once been considered a "cute and innocent" toy, I would **now** classify it in the "violent toys" category.

Why the changes? To answer this, we must consider the people who are creating toys and cartoons today. They are far different from the creators of toys and cartoons of yesteryear. Many of these writers and creators came out of the 60's generation and the drug era, during which they were involved in Eastern religions, such as *Hinduism* and *Buddhism.* Some still are involved in these practices. Many live in Hollywood. Don't misunderstand, I am not saying Hollywood is a "bad place"; but, the very nature of Hollywood leads to a hedonistic way of living, which often involves "meditation," drugs and Eastern religious influences. In line with their lifestyles, most of these cartoon writers and toy designers are not church-going people. Therefore, they are not in tune with their Creator. Finally, many were raised by the *electronic parent* themselves.

Considering their backgrounds, it is easy to understand the influences upon the workings of these writers. While they do not believe that they have been influenced by occult practices, any intelligent person would think otherwise. Hedonistic and Humanistic values have become commonplace and "normal" to them; thus, occult images are revealed in their writings and toy designs. It is impossible to escape what the mind has already absorbed. Since ideas for toys and cartoons come from the mind, if the thoughts are "corrupted," so will the toys and cartoons they design. As a result, many of today's toys and cartoons portray some form of occult images.

Nevertheless, it is not entirely the fault of the writers. Our society consistently is rewarding talent over character. If someone displays genius qualities in the cartoons that he writes or the toys he creates, society rewards him with praise, honor and awards. No one really looks at his character or whether or not he is a "Christian." This is true even among church-going people. For instance, if someone in the church is a good soloist, people tend to focus their attention on the beautiful voice or professional mannerism rather than on that person's spiritual life. As Christians, we need to be more concerned with following God's teachings than on being concerned with how the "world" views us. We must focus on our spiritual lives rather than on our talents. Any talents we have are "God-given" and should not be corrupted with occult ideals. Cartoon writers and toy designers will not change as long as they are rewarded for the things they do, whether or not the products are occult or otherworldly.

I cannot say "Do not buy this toy" or "Do buy that one." It is up to you to decide what is good for your children.

CABBAGE PATCH KIDS

Dolls are generally very good for little girls and boys. They enable children to rehearse the "good parent" role while in their "let's pretend" world. In this sense, *Cabbage Patch Kids* are good. The dolls are soft and large enough for a child. The dolls are also realistic in some ways. Through the doll series, children learn that some children are born prematurely and are smaller than other babies, because this series has regular dolls and *preemies*.

Another doll series, similar to the *Cabbage Patch Kids* series, was introduced at the Toy Fair in New York. This series, *Rice Paddy Babies,* is based on the refugee theme. The dolls, which are created with an Oriental appearance, come with a facsimile of a passport. These dolls received positive reactions from buyers at the Toy Fair.

Although *Cabbage Patch Kids* are a soft, mothering-type doll, they have some disadvantages. I suggest that you consider these disadvantages before deciding that *Cabbage Patch Kids* are appropriate for your children.

In my opinion, the reality surrounding *Cabbage Patch Kids* has been extended *too far.* It is one thing to have a child pretend that a doll is a real baby when playing "house." That is good, because it is based on real life behavior. However, there are many people who forget that the *Cabbage Patch Kid* is just a doll. They view it as "real." They marry them, bury them, and send them off to summer camp. Some even pay to have braces put on the dolls to correct overbites and other dental problems. This is *not* reality. This is an extension of reality that has been taken too far. It is not healthy to view these dolls as real people all the time.

Joyce A Venezia, an Associated Press writer, sent her *Cabbage Patch* doll, Ailienne Julienne, to a two-week prep school and then wrote a news story about it which the AP then transmitted to all participating newspapers.[3] Venezia payed $29.95 for the two-week course at "Patch Prep." The school was begun by Shirley Demetre, a Branford, Conn., housewife, for the "doll who has everything." After two weeks of being "away at school," the doll returns home wearing a school T-shirt sporting the "Patch Prep" logo and carrying a picture of her classmates and a gold-flecked diploma certifying her skill in computers.

Here is another example of people who have extended the dolls' reality too far. It started in the fall of 1984 when one Minnesota mother wanted to clean her daughter's *Cabbage Patch* doll because after "being dragged all over town, to school, play and bed, the doll was losing its sparkle."[4] But the doll's manufacturer warns against putting the doll into the washing machine or having it dry cleaned. After sharing her dilemma with her sisters, the three women developed a cleaning method and launched a "Cabbage Patch Clinic."

For $9.95, *Cabbage Patch* "moms" and "dads" can bring their dolls and similar dolls to the clinic to be washed. The three women also will mend and replace any worn stitching and trim, and if the "mom" or "dad" wants, the women will even style the doll's hair, for no extra charge. The three women promise the "moms" and "dads" that each doll will be washed individually and treated with "tender loving care." Their method? Each doll is washed in a baby tub, dried with baby towels and brushed with baby brushes. One of the three women told a Minnesota reporter, "You really have to take great care when you clean them because you know how much they mean to someone else."[5]

The cleaning process takes five to seven days because the dolls must be completely dry before they are touched. For many children, this is hard. Many of these "moms" and "dads" do not want to leave their "children" at the clinic for that long. "We've seen a lot of tears when the children leave them, but they're all smiles when they come back to pick them up and they're all clean," one of the three women said. "Sometimes they (the children) have to come back to the work area and see what we do and see that there are other babies here so theirs won't be alone. It makes them feel better."[6]

These children no longer view their dolls as dolls, but as real children. Their imaginative play has been extended to the point that it confuses their concept of reality. The line separating their fantasy from the real world has become distorted, fuzzy; they no longer can differentiate between the two.

The manufacturer has contributed to this problem of extending the doll's reality into the real world. Each doll comes with birth certificate and adoption papers. The original dolls, designed by Xavier Roberts, owner of Ozark Artworks, even have birthmarks. Thus, the manufacturer has given the dolls life. When there is a manufacturing defect with the doll, instruction is given to return it to the manufacturer. Unlike other toys, the child simply is not given a refund or replacement. Instead, the manufacturer sends a "death certificate" for the "dead doll." The child then receives a completely different doll, so that the new doll will not look like the "dead" one. In my opinion, this is too advanced for a little child to understand. The end result is that the child's make-believe play becomes unbalanced.

Some people claim that *Cabbage Patch Kids* are good for children because they teach children to be responsible parents. However, I want to emphasize that many of the children who play with these dolls are just four and five years old. They are not mini-adults. Parents should not rush their children into becoming older than what they really are. Because of the "pre-programming" of these dolls, children believe that the dolls are real babies. Children are forced to take on more responsibilities than they can handle at such a young age. You will notice little children in shopping malls carrying dolls. Most of these dolls are *Cabbage Patch Kids,* not ordinary baby dolls. Is it that children play only with *Cabbage Patch Kids* and not ordinary baby dolls? Ordinary baby dolls do not come with the same incentives to treat them like real babies. As a result, little children do not feel guilty about leaving them at home when they go away. But what good mother and father would leave their child home alone unattended? Likewise, children think the same way about their *Cabbage Patch* "babies."

I believe strongly in training children to be responsible adults. Still, I believe that children need to be taught on their own level and not forced to accept more responsibility than they can handle.

Many junior high schools and high schools offer "reality responsibility training" classes, in which students are given a soft-boiled egg and told that, for the next week, this egg is their "baby." The students must care for it like they would a real baby. Wherever they go, the egg must go, unless the student hires a babysitter for the egg. The only time the egg can be out of the student's sight is at night; then, it can be put in the refrigerator while the student sleeps. Several colleges also offer this same training as part of their "Human Services" curriculum. One college student said when she took the class, the egg was raw, not boiled. She said the teacher informed her that if the egg were boiled, it would be the same as "child abuse."

This "responsibility training" concept is not necessarily bad. It teaches that having a family is a big responsibility and it is appropriate for junior high and senior high school students. On the other hand, isn't it carrying the idea too far to tell a little four- or five-year-old girl that a doll is alive and that it has human traits?

Finally, the introduction of *Cabbage Patch Kids* led to a craze. When *Cabbage Patch Kids* first came out in the stores, people were literally stomped while trying to buy the doll. Later, when they became hard to find in stores, there were many classifieds advertising the dolls for more than $100. Regardless of the price, people sought them. The more the interest grew, the more people were insistent that "they had to have one . . . or else." Funny thing is, these people were not only children; many grown women also were fanatical about finding the dolls. Peer pressure among children also mounted, and the dolls became something to acquire because "Suzy had one." The dolls became status symbols, almost to the point of being like an *idol*. The craze fostered a sense of greed among children and taught them how to want things that they did not have. Television, too, teaches greed. The many commercials promoting toys during peak child-viewing times "feed" children with ideas to want those toys, no matter what the cost.

To end my discussion of *Cabbage Patch Kids,* I am not saying these dolls are occult. Yet, I believe these dolls teach young children ideas that are beyond their years. Pre-adolescent children are not ready to become parents; they still have a lot of growing up of their own to do. Why should they be forced to accept the responsibility of really raising a "child"? They should be allowed to play with dolls and pretend that the doll is real; however, that "pretend" should not become confusing for the child. The child should realize that the doll is just a doll and that it does not have human traits.

BARBIE

Barbie dolls and other teenage high-fashion dolls pose a particular threat to younger children. These dolls cause children to develop different attitudes than dolls with which they can practice parenting. These dolls encourage children to focus on self and to strive to meet the ideal perfection that *Barbie* sets forth, such as the perfect hair, body, boyfriend, clothes, car and house.

During the 27 years that the *Barbie* doll has been manufactured by Mattel, she has not added a wrinkle to her face nor an ounce to her remarkable "hourglass" figure. In an interview with *Newsweek* magazine, Bill Barton, a co-designer of the doll in the late 1950s, said, "*Barbie* has become an obsession with little girls."[7] He continued by saying he believes the "bosomy, wasp-waisted" doll can promote unrealistic "beauty expections" in youngsters. "If a child is less attractive, she can develop a psychosis about this," he said. Barton even attributes the current plague of anorexia (self-imposed starvation) in young women partly to *Barbie's* idealized slenderness. "Girls say they want to be as skinny as *Barbie*," he told the *Newsweek* reporter.[8] Barton later confessed he has never given one of the dolls to his young granddaughters. "It seems to me they've put more sex into it now. I like little girls to stay little as long as they can."

A recent review in *People*[9] magazine also mentioned another problem to which *Barbie* could have attributed. In her book *Beauty Bound,* Rita Freedman[10] cautions parents against placing too much emphasis on a little girl's beauty. Children should not grow up thinking that their lives revolve around how well they do in beauty contests, she said. She also said that many beauty-obsessed parents are urging their young teenagers to have breast reductions.

As times have changed, so has *Barbie*. The original doll had stiff hair, pale skin and heavy makeup. Today's *Barbie* is much more mobile and her bustline has appeared to increase slightly, a Mattel spokesman was quoted as saying in the *Dallas Morning News*.[11] *Barbie's* fashions have always mirrored whatever was in style; her hairstyles have ranged from the flower-child look of the 1960s to today's cover-girl look. By the time *Barbie* celebrated her 21st birthday, she had already been Hispanic, Black and Eskimo.[12]

Children become accustomed to these "perfect" ideals that *Barbie* has set forth. When pre-teens play with the doll, they have a firm understanding of fantasy and reality; younger girls do not. Their image of what is "real" is formed from toys and television. This often causes a reality distortion for them; unfortunately, they do not realize their view of reality is distorted. They grow up believing that to get a "good-looking boyfriend" like *Ken,* a girl has to be beautiful like *Barbie.* They also believe that they will own a Corvette sports car and a "dream house." When this fantasy does not materialize, they become disillusioned with life.

Today, more younger girls are playing with *Barbie.* In fact, statistics say more than 330 million *Barbie* dolls so far have been sold.[13] Realizing the potential market among the younger age groups, Mattel has designed a *Barbie* doll specifically for younger girls. The doll is named *My First Barbie.* With this doll, girls of younger ages will be saturated with the "perfection" images these dolls project. Because children will be absorbing these images at a younger and more influential age, the ideals will be further ingrained in their minds by the time they reach their teens. Mattel already has launched a heavy advertising campaign promoting the new doll. One full-page magazine ad shows a little girl, about four years old, playing with the doll. The words accompanying the ad are as follows:

> Remember how you played with your first *Barbie* doll? Changing her clothes, styling her hair—acting out every glamorous fantasy you could dream up?
>
> It's the same with girls today. Except they start playing with *Barbie* dolls at a much younger age than you did. That's why Mattel made a doll called *My First Barbie.* She's specifically designed to be your little girl's very first *Barbie* doll. Here's why *My First Barbie* is simply wonderful:
>
> Her long hair is easy for uncertain little fingers to comb into simple styles. She comes with straight arms. And her straight legs have a special smooth skin—so she's easier for younger girls to dress.
>
> *My First Barbie* comes with a complete easy-to-dress outfit of four fashion pieces to mix or match. And, of course, she has

her own line of *My First Barbie Fashions*! They're all easy-to-dress fashions (each sold separately) that slip on, snap, wrap and tie.

Now, when your little girl is ready for a *Barbie* doll, there's *My First Barbie*. She's the *Barbie* doll that very little hands can handle.

Despite concern that *Barbie* emphasizes physical perfection in an unrealistic manner, Mattel insists that *Barbie* dolls teach some valuable lessons to youngsters, such as fastening seatbelts in the Corvette and good grooming habits.[14]

Children should not grow up *expecting* to be beautiful. Instead, they should be taught that, nationally, very beautiful women make up a very small percentage of the population, and that most women are average but equally accepted in the eyes of God. It should be emphasized that "average" is OK. But it is more important that they focus on their spiritual lives rather than on their physical appearance. It would be far better for the child to play with a regular baby doll and pretend being a mother.

SMURFS

Smurfs are probably one of the most "cute and innocent" of the toys. This is also one in which cartoons have had a tremendous influence on how children see the toy.

The stuffed toys are cute and harmless. On the other hand, when coupled with the *Smurfs* cartoons on Saturday mornings, these toys can help fill the child's minds with occult images. At first, the cartoon appears to be just a cute cartoon. But, behind this facade is a cartoon laden with the occult.

Many forms of the occult are contained in this cartoon. The most obvious display is through the character of *Papa Smurf*. Every time the *Smurfs* have a problem, they go to *Papa Smurf* who whips up a spell or recites an incantation to help them out. These are very strong images to the child's mind. As Christians, we want children to learn to call on the Lord Jesus to help them through problems. In His Word, God tells us to trust Him, and only Him. He tells us not to rely on practices such as witchcraft to solve our problems. Nevertheless, children will not learn Godly principles if they are constantly saturated with images of characters using witchcraft and other occult practices to solve their problems.

The *Smurfs* cartoons also portray characters who are constantly using occult symbols. *In one episode, Gargamel, the evil wizard, drew a pentagram on the floor and lit candles at each point. He then danced within the pentagram while chanting a spell.* The pentagram is a five-pointed star used in the practice of witchcraft. As *Gargamel* finished chanting the spell, a magical book opened across the room. A spirit left the book and entered *Gargamel's* body, giving him power to battle the *Smurfs*. What *Gargamel* did in that episode is what witches have done through the centuries. This is an actual witchcraft practice which millions of children watched. In another episode, *Papa Smurf* used cloves of garlic to counteract a spell that *Gargamel* had placed on the *Smurfs* and their friend.

The child now "knows" how to play with the toy since he knows its abilities, as seen on television. He no longer has to use his imagination to bring the toy to life. This already has been done by the cartoon. He will "visualize" the same situations that he just watched. He will have the toys perform spells and he may even pretend to be the evil *Gargamel*. The more he uses occult practices in his play, the more the occult will become a part of his life. It will no longer seem strange, but will become the norm.

GUMMIE BEARS

Magic, which is so prevalent in the *Smurfs* cartoons, is also a dominant theme in the *Gummie Bears* toy series. There are five *Gummie Bears*, one of which is a magician.

The history of the *Gummie Bears* and their spells are contained in the *Great Book of Gummie*. According to the story, *Gummie Bears* are the descendents of the *Great Gummie Bear*. However, most *Gummie Bears* have lost much of their magical powers because there are such few descendents of the *Great Gummies*. *Gummie Bears* have been brewing *Gummie Berry* juice, which gives humans superhuman powers, for centuries. A little boy befriends the *Gummie Bears*. After drinking the magic juice, he helps them battle the enemies, which are ogres led by an evil, exiled duke.

Although the toys are "cute," the story behind the toys is filled with magic and the occult.

MY LITTLE PONY

My Little Pony has captured the hearts of little children, especially girls, everywhere. Just walk down a toy store aisle, and chances are you will hear a little girl squeal, "Look, Mommy. It's so cute! Can I have one? Pleeeease?"

These little figures are cute. They come in various forms and sizes. The toys are made of a barrage of pastel colors. Some are plastic with combable manes; others are stuffed; and still others are made for the bathtub—they are called *sea horses.* Although many of the horses look like ordinary horses, some are portrayed as unicorns, with horns protruding from their foreheads; others have wings.

Unicorns and winged horses, also known as a *pegasus,* are derived from *Greek and Roman mythology.* Many of the gods are to have owned these mythical creatures. In fact, *Pegasus,* owned by *Bellerophon,* was a winged steed, unwearying of flight, which swept through the air as swift as a gale of wind. It was believed by the Greeks that *Pegasus sprang from Gorgon's blood after Perseus, another mythological character, killed her. Pegasus* received its powers to fly when fitted with a golden bridle. After the death of his master, which *Pegasus* deliberately caused, *Pegasus* went to live in *Zeus's,* god of thunder and lightning, stables. It was *Pegasus's* job to bring the lightning bolts and thunder to *Zeus* whenever he needed them.[15]

Because these toys are based on mythological creatures, they are occult. Mythology is in contradiction to God's Word. That is not the only problem with this series. Unicorns also are a symbol of the *New Age Movement,* which also is in direct contradiction to Scripture. *New Agers* consider the unicorn a symbol of innocence and gentleness personified in the conquering child *Horus.*[16] The Egyptian solar hero is said to conquer through gentility. The *New Age,* also known as the *Golden Age,* is referred to as the Age of Aquarius and the Eon of Horus. Thus, in reality, the unicorn is the symbol of the future conqueror who will bring peace to the earth. **The unicorn is a symbol of the anti-Christ,**[17] **which the prophet Daniel described in his vision as the little horn which rises in the midst of the ten horns.**[18] My Little Pony toys may be cute, but they definitely are based on occult symbolisms. The occult symbolisms are not limited to the toys themselves. The *My Little Pony* cartoon is also laden with the occult.

At first, the cartoon appears cute and innocent. The ponies are playing in a pastel world with green pastures and beautiful springs and brooks. Flying dragons coming down from Heaven with demonic-looking riders interrupt the tranquil scene. The riders' mission is to capture four of the ponies and take them back to the castle by midnight. A creature who is half man/half goat (the cartoon makes a special effort to draw your attention to his cloven hooves) greets the four ponies when they arrive. This creature also has horns protruding from the sides of his head and a bag hanging around his head.

The creature's demonic-looking cohort, named *Scorepan,*

remarks that one of the ponies is too small to pull his *Chariot of Darkness*. The other three ponies are commanded to look into his bag of darkness; as they do so, a power rushes from the bag and transforms the ponies into giant dragons.

Meanwhile, the other ponies in the pasture go to the wizard for help in rescuing their friends. The wizard lives among the mushrooms. (In the drug culture, drug users call a particular hallucinogenic mushroom a "magic mushroom.") The wizard gives the ponies a piece of a rainbow, telling them that the power of the rainbow will help. ***The rainbow is a symbol representing the "New Age Movement."*** Armed with the piece of rainbow, the ponies and a little girl go to the castle, but get caught; one pony is transformed into the last dragon needed to pull the *Chariot of Darkness,* which is to rid the world of goodness.

After seeing the last pony's transformation into a dragon, the little girl throws the piece of rainbow into the air shouting, "The power of the rainbow will defeat you." In response, the half man/half goat creature releases his power of darkness, which forms a black rainbow that overshadows the one released by the little girl. All of a sudden, the little rainbow overpowers the large black one and the spells are broken. The little girl squeals, "You can always depend on the power of the rainbow!"

The above description of one episode is a good example of the intensity and graphics used, which could cause nightmares for the young audience. Yet, this highly frightening cartoon was intended for young children. In addition to the frightening scenes, occult symbolisms and New Age concepts are blatantly portrayed.

CARE BEARS

Care Bears are another example of toys that are acceptable when considered on their own merits. When they are coupled with the movie and two television specials, many parents, especially Christians, find fault with the toys. The elements in contention are not blatantly portrayed in the shows. Instead, they are very subtle. Nevertheless, since there is a considerable amount of interest in the toy series, I will discuss some of the points in contention.

Throughout the *Care Bear* series, there is a subtle interweaving of three ingredients: Humanism, magic, and Eastern religions, which play an intrinsical part in the story lines of the cartoons and books. *Care Bears* are really *Teddy Bears* that share a caring attitude through symbols emblazoned on their tummies. *Care Bears* represent a wide range of human emotions, thus making them appealing to all age groups.

Care Bears live in a world above the clouds, in a land called *Care-A-Lot*. They come to earth whenever they are needed to help children overcome difficult situations and to teach that loving and caring are the most important things in life. Although the *Care Bears'* symbolisms are not Christian, their concept of love and caring is not really incompatible with Jesus' command to love God with our hearts, minds and souls, and to love our neighbors as ourselves.[19] *Care Bears* emphasize feelings, especially the feeling of love. Most of the *Care Bears'* actions are dictated by their feelings. However, the Bible tells us that true love is not based solely on feelings but on commitment. The Humanistic element of our society wants children to base their life and actions on their feelings. In reality, the most miserable people I know are those who have based their lives on their feelings instead of on the Word of God.

In a sense, *Care Bears offer a form of Humanistic psychology, designed to include love, involvement and spontaneity, with the goal of instilling personal growth and the achievement of full human potential.*[20] *Putting it simply,* **Humanism teaches: we are God; there are no ab-**

solutes; and we control our own destiny. This movement has its basis in Eastern religions, such as Buddhism and Hinduism. In line with this, the *bears* teach children to use their feelings to control their lives.[21] As Christians, we know this is not true. The life of the believer is controlled by God and His will. Only He can solve our problems. On the other hand, *Care Bears* play an almost Godlike, or at least an angelic, role when helping out children in trouble and in establishing their own religious order and rituals.

Magic is prevalent in the shows. For instance, a boy becomes obsessed with a magical book from which a demonic entity speaks to him and controls him. He also does sorcery with a magic cauldron. Eastern religious influences are presented throughout the series. The *Care Bears* fight back with their *Care Bear stare,* a power beam that comes from their stomach. Those who practice Eastern religions believe that the person is most powerful when all energy is focused at one central point of the body. The power beam that emanates from the *Care Bears'* stomach is essentially the same concept.

Like so many other toys in this chapter, *Care Bears* are inherently harmless. It is the interweaving of *subtle deception* with which I find fault.

RAINBOW BRITE

Rainbow Brite is a little girl who "can bring sprinkles of color to the darkest day and put a bright smile on a little girl's face."[22] She is a cute little girl. She often is seen gliding through the air on her magical flying horse, *Starlite. Rainbow Brite* and her friends live at the end of the rainbow where all the colors of the earth are created. This sounds very cute and perfect for little girls. But, take another look. This toy and cartoon series is laden with occult symbolisms.

Rainbow Brite lives in *Rainbow Land* with her friends, the *Color Kids,* and *Sprites,* the happy little workers who mine and manufacture *Star Sprinkles*. It is *Rainbow Brite's* job to fight the forces of gloom in order to keep the world bright and filled with color and happiness. In doing so, she often meets horrifying monsters. Although *Rainbow Brite* is fighting for a worthwhile cause, the intensity and violence of these scenes are much more than any five-year-old can handle. Yet, it is for this age group that the cartoons were designed.

The very basis for this series, the *rainbow*, also causes concern for many Christians. Although many people collect rainbows, primarily for their colored beauty, few realize their significance. According to the Word of God, rainbows are a symbol of God's everlasting covenant that He never again would destroy the earth by flood. But for *New Agers*, those who uphold the tenets of the *New Age Movement* or *Humanism*, the rainbow holds a different meaning. *New Agers* use "rainbows to signify their building of the 'Rainbow Bridge' (antahkarana) between man and Lucifer who, they say, is the over-soul."[23]

Children today are filled with Humanistic teachings at school. In fact, Humanism has become so commonplace in our lives, that we fail to recognize the occult symbolisms that are the root of these tenets. Nevertheless, Humanism is contradictory to God's Word. Thus, any toy or cartoon series that employs symbolisms from the *New Age Movement* is also in contradiction to Scripture.

After reading this chapter, it is hoped that you have gained a better understanding of some of the subtle means that Satan uses to take control of a child's mind. Remember, that which, on the surface, may appear to be "cute and innocent" is not always "cute and innocent!"

9

MASTERS OF THE UNIVERSE

He is strong, handsome and all-powerful. He is the "Master of the Universe." He is "He-Man." For many children, he has become a God-like figure. Someone who can solve any problem with might. He never loses a battle and is always there to help when a friend is in trouble. Children see him as omnipotent and omniscient.

Mattel created the *Masters of the Universe* toy series in 1982. But sales did not begin to skyrocket until after the introduction of the half-hour daily cartoon series in the fall of 1983. In fact, *He-Man and the Masters of the Universe* cartoon series was the first cartoon to be designed specifically for syndication on independent stations.[1] All three major networks refused to show the series. As of December, 1984, the show is seen weekdays on 166 television stations in the United States and in 37 foreign countries. Since its debut, the cartoon has gained an audience of nearly nine million children in the United States alone, making it reportedly the number one children's show in syndication.[2] According to the show's executive producer, Lou Scheimer, although *He-Man and the Masters of the Universe* is most popular with boys between four and eight years old, 30 percent of the viewers are girls.[3]

The cartoon series is based on the plastic "action figures" that Mattel created in 1982. Since their introduction until

December, 1984, the toy company had sold 70 million of these action figures worldwide; 55 million of these were sold in the United States. This averages out to be 1.7 for every American child who is nine years old or younger, according to David Capper, marketing director for boys' toys for the company.[4] Capper reports that if the action figures were lined single file, they would stretch from Los Angeles to New York and back. Only the *Barbie* doll, which has current annual sales of more than $260 million, has had a similar appeal in Mattel's history.[5]

It has been reported that "*He-Man* power has sold $500 million in toys made by the Mattel Co. for its *Masters of the Universe* line and another $500 million in *He-Man* toothbrushes, underwear, sheets, towels and alarm clocks manufactured under license to Mattel."[6] This means that total sales of all *He-Man and Masters of the Universe* products have topped the $1 billion mark for Mattel.

That is a considerable amount of toys sold when we consider the six-inch action-figure dolls sell for only $5 and the accessories, such as vehicles and a replica of *Castle Grayskull* which doubles as a carrying case, sell for $20 and more. Still, after just a few years on the market, sales are mushrooming. It has been reported that *He-Man* sales account for 50 percent of Mattel's gross sales. Even a company spokesman said that the *He-Man* toys in particular get snapped up as soon as toy stores can get them on the shelves.[7]

Many toy store managers say the popularity of the *Masters of the Universe* series rivals the popularity of the *Cabbage Patch Kids*. Parents say the toys are especially hard to find during *Christmas* and *Hannukah* holiday seasons. Consider this scene at a Macy's department store in mid-December: A dozen anxious parents reportedly became upset and berated some of the clerks after *He-Man* figures were put on the shelves and then quickly taken down again because they had been priced incorrectly. Managers of toy stores in metropolitan areas say they can barely keep the toys in stock. Parents drive for miles to buy them and trade tips with other parents on where to find the collection's newest characters.[8]

There are more than two dozen different action figures, both good and bad. Most of the figures twist at the waist so they can be more easily engaged in combat with each other while the child plays with them. Each year, the company adds new toys to the series to keep pace with the interest and demand. In fact, a 12-year-old Illinois boy won $100,000 in Mattel's *Create-A-Character* contest in December, 1985.[9] The toy he designed, *Fearless Photog,* who captures enemies on film and drains them of their evil tendencies, will become part of the *Masters of the Universe* line in 1987. Also, as part of the contest, the child will be appointed "honorary president" for a day and be consulted on the company's 1986 products.

Why the mass appeal? Why is this cartoon and toy series so popular? For one thing, before the *Masters of the Universe* cartoon series was introduced, most of the shows on television during afterschool hours were reruns. Consequently, when the series debuted, it attracted children's interest because it was something new and exciting. Once children started watching the show, the cartoons maintained their interest with the characters' adventures. Each half-hour show is filled with the characters displaying supernatural powers.

But the characters in the series are not like characters in any other cartoon or toy series. These are different. They are unusual. These characters are a mixture of the ancients, computerization and mutants. This series borrows ideas from mythological stories and interweaves them with the modern computerization age. As a result, the characters often resemble mutants—half man and half beast, or half man and half robot. All of these characters play almost God-like roles. Often, they take control of a situation with their powers. Also, the setting of the series is in the unknown mystical world of *Eternia,* where the past, present and future seem to run together. Anytime an unknown world is the setting of a show, it holds a certain fascination for viewers. It provides an extension to their fantasy play. After viewing just a few episodes, it is easy to see how the show was influenced by *Superman, Conan the Barbarian, Star Wars, Greek and Roman mythology* and *King Arthur's Knights of the Round Table legends.*

In addition to attracting children, the show has reportedly pleased many parents and educators by placing simple moral messages at the end of each story. Whatever the day's storyline, there is always a "pro-social" message, such as being responsible for one's actions and the importance of friendship, teamwork and cooperation, that is drawn from the story, not merely tacked on at the end. However the moral of the story generally takes about 37 seconds. That does not exactly make a half-hour show balanced, especially on some of the more violent and occult episodes. Some also say the show is less violent than other cartoon series. This point is hotly debated by others—the show averages 37 violent scenes for every half-hour episode.

The star of the cartoon and toy series is *He-Man.* Actually, *He-Man* is the alter-ego of a blonde, Herculean prince named *Adam,* who is prince of the planet *Eternia.* When trouble arises, *Adam* points his sword aloft and shouts, *"by the power of Grayskull, I have the power!"* Magically, he turns into *He-Man,* the most powerful man in the universe, amid much smoke and lightning. At the same time, *Adam's* feline pet *Cringer* metamorphosizes into a mighty horse-sized *Battle Cat.*

The primary role of *He-Man* is to defend the secrets of the universe, housed in *Castle Grayskull,* from the evil *Skeletor* and his legion of villains. *He-Man* is aided in his efforts by his friends, *Man-at-Arms, Teela* and *Orko*. *He-Man's* arch enemy *Skeletor* is a super-powered villain. Most episodes revolve around the attempts of *Skeletor* and his crew, including *Beastman, Evil-Lyn, Trap Jaw* and *Tri-Klops,* to enslave *Eternia* or at least capture the castle.

After the shows, which are actually half-hour commercials for the toys, are over, the children go to the toy box and take out their *Masters of the Universe* toys and act out their fantasies. Some children imitate exactly what they have just seen the characters on television do. Others act out fantasy games of their own. This should concern parents because of the occult images portrayed. Because of their age, the children do not realize that their actions are conveying occult images.

Children see that the *power of Grayskull* transforms *Adam* into a character with supernatural powers and abilities. **Many parents have expressed concern that their children, after watching the "He-Man" cartoons, go running throughout the house with plastic swords held aloft shouting, "by the power of Grayskull, I have the power!"** God's Word warns us that only by the blood of Jesus do humans have any power and authority over others. There is no mention of the *power of Grayskull.*

Before we discuss other occult images presented in the series, let me share with you a letter that one man wrote me a few months ago. This letter is filled with concern over the effects that the *He-Man* series was having on the man's children.

Dear Phil:

I want to share with you some guidelines which I have developed for use with our children in deciding which programs and toys are appropriate for our children. This is always the problem, isn't it? We know we must restrict the material available to our children but which items should we restrict? This is a difficult decision especially with "borderline" items. Unfortunately I have few opportunities to watch children's shows due to my schedule. When I do have an opportunity to watch, however, I now ask myself a simple question: ***"Is there a place for Jesus in this story?"*** If the answer is "No," then my answer to my children is "No."

I wish I had known about this technique when *He-Man* first came out. This show has been barred from our home for a year now. I was upset with the effect it was having on my two boys. They seemed to be constantly fighting with friends and each other. Worse still was their "zombie-like" attitude. Our eldest son would wait all day for the half-hour when *He-Man* came on, lost in aggressive fantasies. Believe it or not, our third son's first words were *"I have the power."* When I placed the show off-limits, they protested mildly. After a few days, we were sure we had made the right decision. The level of hostility decreased greatly and they actually began to *play* again, not just wait for *He-Man*. Incidentally, Phil, we have always restricted the total amount of TV viewing to a maximum of three programs a day.

If I had known to ask "Is there a place for Jesus in this story?" I never would have let my sons watch *He-Man* as long as they did. Jesus obviously would not have been acceptable to *He-Man's* enemy *Skeletor,* but he would, I believe, find no home with the "good guys" in the show. I believe that *He-Man* fights only for dominance and ego gratification and that he fights only in self-defense. . . . But, the society that he defends is purely Humanistic, pagan, unleavened by Christian love.

Other elements found in *He-Man* and other such shows are the use of sorcery and magic (there is a character in *He-Man* called the *Sorceress*), and the presence of what we might call "composite creatures," half man/half animal and half man/half robot. I know there is no place for Jesus in such a society which so debases the image and likeness of God. I object to any show with aspects which tend to blur the distinction between good and evil. Many of the children's shows are promoting the Humanist ethos: there is no right or wrong; everything is relative; it all depends on your perspective. . . .

A Christian Brother

This letter is just one example of many that demonstrates that children do in fact re-enact what they see on television when they play with their toys. As you know, they will use their imagination to bring the same life to the toys that the characters displayed in the cartoon.

My first objection to this cartoon and toy series is the "implied message." The name, *Masters of the Universe,* implies that these characters are superior to humans and that they are on the same plane as God. ***But there is only one God and He alone is the Ruler and "Master of the universe."*** Thus, the implication of their superiority is blasphemous. They are not God. Still, children today lift up *He-Man* as the children of Israel lifted up and worshipped pagan gods.

The series, both cartoons and toys, blatantly use occult symbols in various forms. *Castle Grayskull,* through which *He-Man* receives his powers, has its own spirit which manifests itself in the form of a skull. This manifestation is seen often in the comics that accompany the dolls as well as in the cartoons.

The chief promoter of the occult in the series is *Skeletor,* also known as *Lord of Destruction.* He is *He-Man's* arch enemy. *Skeletor,* whose face is actually a skull, carries a ram's head staff. This staff, which is used in occult practices, often is seen with a dove crushed underneath it. *Skeletor* also has the power to astro-project himself and to read and control other people's minds. This ability often is practiced by mediums. In Deuteronomy 18:10-12 and also in Galatians 5:19-21, God warns against those who practice these powers. God says these practices are detestable to Him, and anyone who does such things will not inherit the kingdom of God.

In the comic book *Power of Point Dread,* which accompanies one of the figures, *Skeletor* is seen levitating himself in a classic "lotus position"—with his legs crossed, palms out and resting on his knees; a power beam, coming from his head, levitates a crystal ball. The crystal ball is used in necromancy, which is communication with the dead.[10] This form of worship can still be seen today in the Asian country of Tibet, where Tibetan monks have been known to levitate themselves 100 feet in the air and travel more than a quarter of a mile.

In the *Magic Stealer* comic book, *Skeletor* introduces the pyramid cult, which is the power of the pyramid. In this same comic, the "maddened spirits of the air" attack *He-Man*.[11] Are these the practices we want our children to imitate when they play? Do we really want our children to learn to do things *by the power of Grayskull?* Or do we want our children to know that God is the real "Master of the Universe" and that through His power all things are possible?

Occult symbolisms, however, do not stop with *Skeletor. Teela,* who the series refers to as a "warrior goddess," carries a cobra head staff. Her helmet and breastplate also are made in the likeness of a cobra. In many countries, the cobra is worshipped as a god.

"We are created in the image of God;" yet, the *Master of the Universe* series has distorted and debased this truth by creating mutants. (A mutant is any creature which has undergone some changes to make it unlike any other creature in its species.) Some of the mutants are as follows:

Man-E-Faces—a human, robot and monster.
Beast Man—a savage henchman. He is half man and half beast.
Stratos—a winged warrior. He is half man and half bird.
Mer-Man—ocean warlord. He is half man and half reptile.
Tri-Klops—sees everything. He has only one eye in the center of his forehead.

Mattel did not stop with the creation of *He-Man* and the rest of the *Masters of the Universe* series. This company also captured the imagination and interests of little girls by creating *She-Ra,* also known as *Princess of Power.*

She-Ra also has a toy and cartoon series. As in the *Masters of the Universe* series, the action figures come with little comic books that are laden with the occult.

The story is told that *She-Ra* is really *Adora,* the twin sister of *Adam,* otherwise known as *He-Man.* However, when *Adora* was little, she was kidnapped from the castle in *Eternia* and taken to live in *Etheria,* a planet ruled by the evil *Hordak.* Years later, *Adora* and *Adam* were reunited. It was then that Adora was given the magic *Sword of Protection.* While holding the *Sword of Protection* aloft, *Adora* shouted, *"By the honor of Grayskull, I am She-Ra."* Amid smoke and lightning *Adora* was transformed into *She-Ra,* the most powerful woman in the universe. While *Adora* is under the power of *Grayskull,* her white horse *Spirit* is metamorphosized into a magical flying unicorn known as *Swift Wind.*[12]

This series also is filled with occult practices and characters. *She-Ra* is befriended by *Kowl,* an owl-like creature who knows everything. In this manner, *Kowl* is similar to a warlock. *Kowl* also casts spells. The *Voice of the Unknown* is the voice of *Etheria's* past and the seer of its future.

Shadow Weaver is another character who introduces much of the occult into the series. *Shadow Weaver* is an evil witch who works for *Hordak.* In one story, *Shadow Weaver* transforms herself into a little girl who comes to *Etheria* to participate in a witches' spell-casting contest. During the contest, *She-Ra* comes in to try herself. While *She-Ra* is there, the little girl (who is really *Shadow Weaver*) comes in and asks to try. Through her spells, the little girl makes all of *She-Ra's* friends go to sleep and sends *She-Ra* to the *Sixth Dimension,* which is down in a pit. These spells that the little girl casts are very specific and in depth. In fact, they are similar to spells that would be found in a book on witchcraft.

There are two characters in the series which Mattel describes in a similar manner to "angels" and "Jesus." *Angella* is described in the comic books that accompany the action figures as *an angelic winged guide. Glimmer* is described as *a guide who lights the way.* This is similar to how, *in the Gospels, Jesus says, "I am the Way, the Truth and the Light."* With these comics, children are filled with images of magical creatures serving roles similar to Jesus and angels.

These children see *She-Ra* and *He-Man* as being all-powerful, God-like. Then, when the children need help, many parents say the children call on *He-Man* and *She-Ra* to "save" them. Remember the example given earlier about the little boy who was comforting his mom after they nearly had a car accident? "Don't worry, Mommy, *He-Man* would have saved us." Children must be taught that God, alone, is all-powerful. Most importantly, children must be made aware that these characters are not real.

The seeds of *subtle deception* were planted in the shows and books, but the child's own imagination waters the seed until it grows into a fascination of the occult. Some parents may think it is cute when their children play in this manner. How cute will they think these very same actions are when the child is a teen and is involved in actual occult practices? Through these cartoons and toys, an unconscious fascination of the occult begins to form.

GLOSSARY OF TERMS[13]

He-Man—most powerful man in the universe.
Man-E-Faces—heroic human, robot, monster.
Zoar—fighting falcon.
Ram Man—heroic human, battering ram.
Trap Jaw—evil and armed for combat.
Tri-Klops—evil and sees everything.

Skeletor—Lord of Destruction.
Battle Cat—fighting tiger.
Castle Grayskull—fortress of mystery and power.
Spirit of the Castle—manifested by a gray skull.
Teela—warrior goddess.
Power Sword—He-Man's source of power.
Stratos—a winged warrior.
Delora—human wife of Stratos.
Man-at-Arms—master of weapons.
Emerald Staff—gives the bird people the power to fly.
Snake Mountain—where Skeletor lives.
Haramesh and **Orcs**—demons.
Masks of Power—whoever wears these gains tremendous strength to use for good or evil.
Mer-Man—ocean warlord.
Beast Man—savage henchman.
Zodac—cosmic enforcer.
Secret Liquid of Life—holds the secret to eternal life.
Magic Siphon—a device used by Skeletor to absorb all the magic from Eternia.
Mists of Sight—sorceress' magic window to the world.
She-Ra—most powerful woman in the universe.
Bow—She-Ra's special friend.
Double Trouble—glamorous double agent.
Frosta—ice empress.
Catra—jealous beauty.
Castaspella—enchantress who hypnotizes.
Kowl—the know-it owl.
Angella—angellic winged guide.
Glimmer—guide who lights the way.
Hordak—ruthless leader of the evil Horde.
Swift Wind—She-Ra's magical flying unicorn.
Voice of the Unknown—the voice of Etheria's past and the seer of its future.
Sword of Protection—sword through which She-Ra gains her powers.
Light Hope—She-Ra's powerful friend who lives at the bottom of a mysterious pool in the castle.
Shadow Weaver—an evil witch.
Madame Razz—200-year-old magical woman.

PICTURE SECTION: The following pages contain a representative sampling of the toys discussed throughout this book. The pictures of the toys, magazine advertisements, movie and cartoon characters, and posters are intended to better aquaint the reader with the actual products.

Cabbage Patch Graduating Class

Care Bear Stare (power beam)

Facsimile of an Advertisement
(from a trade magazine to the toy industry)

Now we're monstrous and gross, too.

You know the marketing and creative reputation of Those Characters From Cleveland. Now we're doing it again.

Meet My Pet Monster™ and Madballs™!

My Pet Monster is super-size and tough, but he's also a best pal for boys. And he's two toys in one, because his breakaway chains come off so his owner can bust loose, too. My Pet Monster is comin' at ya with a multi-million dollar TV campaign. How's that for monstrous excitement!

Madballs are gross fun for everyone — especially boys. Because with Madballs, boys can gross out their friends, play ball, and collect 'em, too. Madballs are sweeping the country. And there'll be millions in TV advertising this Spring to keep them grossly successful.

My Pet Monster and Madballs are already hot. They could be naturals in your product line, too. Get the whole story from Greg Miller at Those Characters From Cleveland.

THOSE CHARACTERS FROM CLEVELAND
An American Greetings Company

Ram Man (extended)

Ram Man (ramming)

Beast Man (savage henchman)

Masters of the Universe

War & Violence

Black Star Group
(note the two glow-in-the-dark alien demons)

Star Wars — Darth Vader

**Power Lords—Shea
(humanoid form)**

**Power Lords—Shea
(extra-terrestrial form)**

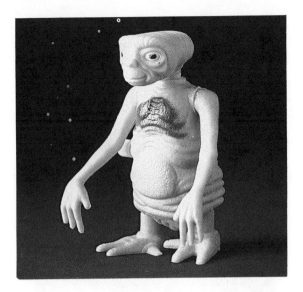

E.T.

Star Wars — Yoda

G.I. Joe

Dungeons & Dragons Poster

Dungeons & Dragons — Orkian Assassin

Pegasus & Unicorn
(mixed)

Jesus Christ Crucified on a Pentagram
(from a comic book)

Robotech

ThunderCats

Rainbow Brite

HASBRO MAKES IT HAPPEN!

THE MOST INNOVATIVE FASHION DOLL CONCEPT IN THE LAST 25 YEARS!!

Facsimile of an Advertisement
(from a trade magazine to the toy industry)

BARBIE

REMEMBER
WHEN
TOYS
WERE
TOYS?

10

THE BARBARIZATION OF OUR CHILDREN

Toys and games promoting violence and occult practices are growing in popularity. In 1985, the National Coalition on Television Violence reported that war toys comprise the leading category of toy sales in the United States.[1] The coalition also reported that a cartoon series promoting the most popular of these toys was also the most violent.

Since 1982, sales of war toys have climbed by 350 percent to a record $842 million per year.[2] *Transformers,* a series of futuristic robot warriors, are the most popular war toys. The *Transformers* cartoon series averages 83 acts of violence, making it the most violent cartoon on television. Other violent toys on the "best-seller" list include *Masters of the Universe, GoBots, Voltron* and *G.I. Joe*—all of which are promoted by violent cartoons, according to the coalition.

In addition to the violent cartoons, it is estimated that in 1985 the average American child saw 800 advertisements promoting violent toys.[3] Violent cartoons bombard children with images that make violence appear fun and harmless. These acts of aggression are bound to affect a child's behavior. Do we want children to believe that guns and sorcery are an important part of everyday life? Since children view television as reality, do we want them growing up thinking that "*good guys* never get hurt in battle"? Do we want them to believe that aggression is an acceptable means to settle disputes? These possibilities are not far-fetched. Many children actually grow up believing these myths.

Many parents believe children should be allowed to "dabble in the evil of the world," such as with violent and occult toys and shows, because they want their children to experience "reality." Peer pressure also is a major influence. Parents do not want to deprive their children of experiences and material goods that their friends might have.[4] Although the real world is violent, filled with murders, Satanism and the occult, Christians should not expose their children unnecessarily to these unGodly acts. Children must live in the world and they will be exposed to violence at some time in their life. Nevertheless, should we invite violence and the occult into our homes to be a part of our children's play time? Christ tells us in John 15:19 that *Christians are not of the world because He has chosen us out of the world.*

Scripture also warns believers against associating with unbelievers. In II Corinthians 6:14,16-17, Paul says "*Do not be mismated with unbelievers. For what partnership have righteousness with iniquity? Or what fellowship has light with darkness? What agreement has the temple of God with idols? For we are the temple of the living God; as God said, 'I will live in them and move among them, and I will be their God, and they shall be my people. Therefore come out from them, and be separate from them, says the Lord, and touch nothing unclean; then I will welcome you . . .*'" (RSV). This same principle can be applied to toys that our children play with. Christian children should not be associated with toys and games that feature occult philosophies and phenomena because they glorify Satan and his battle against the church. Matthew 6:24 states: *No man can serve two masters: for either he will hate the one and love the other; or else he will hold to the one, and despise the other. Ye cannot serve God and mammon.* By encouraging our children to play with violent and occult toys, we are serving Satan, while at the

114

same time trying to serve God. We cannot do both. Jesus warns in Matthew 12:25 of the dangers of attempting to serve two masters: *"Every kingdom divided against itself is laid waste, and no city or house divided against itself will stand"* (RSV).

Any toy representing violence or associated with occult practices should be prohibited from Christian homes. Violent toys enable children to rehearse violent behavior which is seen on television and in movies. This increases the likelihood that they will incorporate these violent scenes into their "let's pretend" world and later into their everyday life. University of Utah's Charles Turner asserts in the *Journal of Experimental Child Psychology* that "playing with violent toys increases the risks that children are going to use aggression in real life at a later time."[5]

An item in a recent advice column, written by Dr. Joyce Brothers, focuses on effects of war toys on children.[6] A concerned parent wrote Dr. Brothers, a well-known psychologist. This letter is not unusual. Today, more parents are concerned that toys promoting violence are causing a growing hostility among children. They fear these toys are causing heightened aggression among their children's siblings and peers. Following is the letter written to Dr. Brothers.

> Dear Dr. Brothers:
> My brother is a Marine and he has bought our five-year-old son a number of war toys. My husband objected because he says he doesn't want our son growing up thinking that killing people off is all part of being a man.
> I don't want to hurt my brother's feelings, but I don't particularly like having my son playing with these either. Are they harmful?

Dr. Brothers agrees war toys can be harmful. "It would be foolish to think that war toys are going to help children be cooperative, loving and gentle. They also don't help children solve problems in a constructive way," she answered.[7] Dr.

Brothers emphasized that many war toys are exact copies of actual weapons. Because these toys look like actual weapons, she says they remind children that adults often settle disputes with force and violence. Is this what we want our children to learn?

According to Dr. Brothers, various studies have shown a link between a child's playing with war toys and his exhibiting of aggressive behavior, such as hyperactivity, kicking, biting, punching and general rule-breaking.[8] Is this the type of behavior we want to encourage in our children?

Despite parents' concern, toy companies are not suffering. In fact, as mentioned earlier, sales have increased by 350 percent in the last four years. Psychiatrist Dr. Thomas Radecki is quoted in Dr. Brothers' column as saying this is the "most massive sale of war ideology to a generation of children in any modern nation with the exception of Hitler's Germany."[9]

These toys and games are "worrisome" for many reasons. Many involve techno-violence; others are laden with human violence and still others are totally occult.

Techno-violence toys are similitudes of robots. Some of these possess occult power, specifically the ability to alter material objects through force of will. This ability suggests intelligence and the ability to reason and act on free will. These characteristics, however, are normally reserved for God, man, angels and demons. With these characteristics, there generally exists a spirit, which suggests the Eastern mystical concept of a universal "life-force" is true. Although not all techno-violence toys are associated with occult power, they are intrinsically linked to violence for violence's sake. This prepares children to believe that science and technology are the ultimate powers in the universe.[10] Some of the more popular techno-violence toys include *GoBots*, *Transformers*, *Voltron*, *Robotech*, *Powerboats*, *Wheeled Warriors*, *MASK* and *Spectaurs*. Most of these toys are associated with cartoons and are discussed in the *Commercialtoons* chapter.

Human violence toys are those made in the image of men who exhibit raw, human strength to overpower others. Many of these toys have only one purpose: to simulate the act of killing other humans. Some of the more popular toys in this category are *Wrestling Superstars* and *G.I. Joe.*

Toys and games based solely on occult practices include *Dungeons and Dragons, Crystlar, Black Star* and *Power Lords.* These toys and games feature characters performing magic, sorcery and other occult practices, as well as having certain "powers" over others, especially demons. Many of the spells and magic used are described in books of witchcraft.

Toys in these three categories are "worrisome," or at least they should arouse concern with parents. They teach values that most of us would not want our children to learn, let alone practice.

Why the popularity? What is so attractive about these toys that leads to such a fascination among boys? Children's fascination with these "worrisome" toys is not limited to *G.I. Joe* and other similar toys and cartoons. *Rambo,* which is considered an extremely violent movie, has attracted many children. *Rambo* and other similar movies are "Rated R;" yet, dozens of children can be seen at theaters watching them. As a result, they are having an effect on children. Some say these movies add patriotism to America; they say that it shows a revival in American patriotism. I see that revival as ***"barbarianism," not "patriotism."***

Violent movies teach that *every* problem should be handled with a gun or sword. I am not a pacifist by any means, but the portrayal of war in these movies is grossly misconstrued. They portray war as fun; they give the impression that *good guys* never get hurt or lose. These movies desensitize children to pain and violence by showing

117

thousands of violent acts. It is bound to have an effect on the way children view war. War is glorified; war is fun. However, anyone who has ever been in a real war will tell a different story—one that children today never hear.

I recently heard a reporter say that Russia is not so concerned about the nuclear weapons that the United States has built up, as they are about our children walking around in Army fatigues. They are very worried about this new attitude in America. When you think about it, this is a cause of alarm for them (Russians), because they barbarize their children and they understand the power in it.

Some people deny that children really believe these attitudes on violence and war. They deny that children are desensitized to acts of aggression. But, many parents tell me they do see a "barbarization" of today's youth, and they are concerned. Parents worry about the types of adults children will become. Consider the following anecdote about a family who visited the Toy Fair in New York. The names are fictitious, but the story is real. Are these children much different from yours?

> In a world of sex-stereotyped toys for boys and girls, Johnny and Jenny are a toymaker's dream.
>
> Johnny, 9, loves playing war with his *G.I. Joe, Transformers* and *GoBots*. His favorite color is blue.
>
> Jenny, 5, loves to cuddle her *Cabbage Patch Preemies, Rainbow Brite* toys and *Care Bears*. Her favorite color is pink.
>
> While visiting the annual trade show unveiling what manufacturers hope will be "hot toys" this year, Johnny and Jenny wanted to buy everything.
>
> Johnny was a pushover when it came to critiquing Coleco's new line of *Rambo* action figures. "Oh, cool," he said as he eyed a nearly seven-inch doll outfitted with a Uzi machine gun and an anti-tank grenade.
>
> His excitement was hard to control when he saw *Mad Dog,* one of the bad guys from the *Secret Army of Vengeance and Global Evil. Mad Dog* was wearing studded wristbands and armed for battle with a fast-draw shotgun.

Jenny and Mom were not as pleased with the toys as Johnny was.

"I don't encourage him to have guns," Mom said. "This is all a bit too frightening." She noticed that the showroom had enough miniature hardware for a child to wage a "play global war."

"I like the violence," Johnny replied, his fists rolled into a punch. "I'm going to buy one whether she'll let me or not. I'll use my own money."

Jenny was most impressed with the *Cabbage Patch Kids* and accessories.

Although these toys interested Johnny some, he did not show too much enthusiasm. Johnny's enthusiasm did not mount again until he saw *Tonka's* new *Rock Lords*, transformable action figures that start out looking like boulders.

"Toys that don't transform are sometimes boring," he replied.

Late that afternoon as the tired threesome were leaving, Johnny wondered aloud, "What are they going to think of next? How about a *Rambo Cabbage Patch Kid?*"

The "mom" is not much different in her thinking from other parents. It is scary that "Johnny" could be so barbarized that he would think it would be nice to have a *Rambo Cabbage Patch Kid. Cabbage Patch Kids* are one of the most "cute and innocent" appearing toys on the market, but "Johnny" wants to add violence to even these "cute" dolls. This is indeed cause for alarm—not just for Russia, but for adults everywhere.

Some of the more "worrisome" toys will be discussed in detail in this chapter. Remember, several toys that would be considered "worrisome," including *Transformers, Black Star* and *G.I. Joe,* will not be discussed in this chapter because they were presented in the chapter on cartoons. *Masters of the Universe* and *Dungeons and Dragons* are discussed in chapters of their own.

CRYSTLAR

The *Saga of the Crystlar Warrior* action figures include so much of the occult it almost becomes redundant. Here is an excerpt from the back of toy's box: **Somewhere in the universe exists Crystalium, a world where magic reigns! After a cosmic demon war, twin brothers, Crystar and Moltar, became rulers of Crystalium.**

The brothers have to choose between order and chaos, which bears a similarity to *Zen Buddhism,* and they are transformed into superhuman creatures by the mystical powers of wizards. The crystal, as seen here, is used in the occult practice of necromancy, the practice of talking with the dead.

This toy series' use of the occult is enough to make it "worrisome." The Lord warns in Deuteronomy 18:10-12 that these acts are detestable to him. And in Galatians, Paul tells us that anyone found practicing such beliefs will not inherit the kingdom of God.

POWER LORDS

The name of this toy line causes concern. The name implies that these figures are equal in power to God. In the Word, God tells us that He is the only Lord. On the other hand, these characters are called *Power Lords,* making them equal to God. This is blasphemous.

This group of action figures is one of the most gruesome on the market. They portray a transformation of the body into beast-like characters. The manufacturer describes *Shaya,* the power queen, in this quote: "*Shaya, queen of power,* is a changer. She has cosmic might equal to Adam's powers. When in danger, she is capable of changing from humanoid to extra-terrestrial. Her alien form gives off an intense heat which repels her enemies." This set of action figures also includes *Arkus,* the evil dictator; *Raygoth,* the goon of doom; and *Gapplog,* the four-fisted brute.

Like *Crystlar,* this toy series employs occult practices. These grotesque characters possess powers that enable them to change forms. In Genesis, however, the Lord tells us He created us in His image.

GARBAGE PAIL KIDS

Topps Gum Co. recently released a new line of trading cards in their packs of gum. They are *Garbage Pail Kids,* and they are a satirical portrayal of the *Cabbage Patch Kids.* These children are ugly and grotesque. Nevertheless, they have created quite a fervor among youngsters.

On a recent network news show, it was reported that a public school in New York City banned the *Garbage Pail Kids* cards from being displayed during school hours. The principal and faculty believed the cards were causing a disturbance among the students. Any cards found in the school are confiscated. Needless to say, the students were upset. Most could not understand the fuss about these "cute" cards. Some agreed the cards were "ugly, but still cute." "They're hot!" one girl told a reporter.

These cards do not picture little babies doing cute things. Instead, they show babies whose heads are being decapitated by a guillotine; babies smoking cigarettes; and another of a baby whose arms and legs have been cut off and scattered on the floor. Cute? There is also one called *Ray Decay. Ray* is portrayed as he gorges on junk food. He only has two teeth—both are completely rotted. *Dead Ted* shows a badly decomposing boy rising from a grave.

On the other side of these trading cards, the child gets an added treat—certificates that they can award to their friends. Here is one example:

STUPID STUDENT AWARD

Although you used to be a clumsy little jerk you outgrew this—now you're a clumsy BIG jerk. You were the most popular student in the sixth grade—for five straight years! Every medical school wants you, but not while you're alive.

Signed by A.B. Dummy, the Commissioner of D.C.A. (Dumb Clucks of America)

Do these toys foster the love and friendship that Jesus stresses so often in the Bible? These toys are a mockery of everything that is cute and innocent. It is disturbing that children could even like such grotesque toys.

VOODOO REAGAN DOLLS

New *Ronald Reagan voodoo dolls* are being sold with stickpins and a vicious incantation to put a hex on the President. Buyers are encouraged to stick pins into the three-color, 11-inch styrofoam doll as they chant a curse. God's name is used to complete the curse, the last two lines of which are an actual voodoo hex. Although the firm which is marketing the doll, The Force, claims that the doll and curse are all in fun, God forbids the use of enchantment in Leviticus 19:26,31 and 20:6,27.

GOLDEN GIRL

Galoob's Golden Girl and the *Guardians of the Gemstones* represents the first time an adventure/fantasy line has been developed specifically for little girls. The line features 11 action figures, combining fantasy/adventure with doll play: *Golden Girl, Jade, Rubee, Saphire, Onyx, Prince Kroma, Dragon Queen, Moth Lady, Wild One, Vultura* and *Ogra Bad Guy*. In addition to various outfits, the dolls come with weapons and shields for action and adventure.

It seems toy companies are not satisfied with "barbarizing" little boys. Now, they are encouraging little girls to develop a fascination with violence and war. An added twist to the doll's accessories: the weapon and die-cast shield can be worn as a brooch. The danger of these objects are lessened when seen as jewelry.

BUILD A GUILLOTINE

Perigree Books recently released a series of cut-and-assemble books called *The Way Things Work*. These books are not the average "how-to-do-it" books. They describe how to make working models of guillotines and catapults.

Early editions of the guillotines included a cardboard figure that children could have fun decapitating. More recent editions have this conclusion: "And now you're all finished. Strap in a small toy soldier, turn the handle, and let the blade fall. See how a guillotine actually works."

Imagine parents allowing their children to play with such a thing. With this toy, there is always the possibility that one child may try to decapitate a sibling. In John 13:34, Jesus gives a new commandment: ". . . That ye love one another; as I have loved you, that ye also love one another." He does not encourage fighting, let alone decapitating. Instead, "But I say unto you, That ye resist not evil: but whosoever shall smite thee on thy right cheek, turn to him the other also."[11]

GODBOX

A Carson City, Nev., company claims it has a direct line to God through its *Godbox*. The $14.95 wooden box is designed to relay the owner's prayers directly to God's care, according to Jerry Goossen of A Creative Co., makers of the *Godbox*. Included in the promotional materials are testimonials from people whose prayers were answered through use of the box. But it is hard to tell whether it was God or the *Godbox* who answered.

This toy is definitely blasphemous. The creators would have children believe that a box could actually have a "direct line to God." God tells us we do not need an intermediate person or thing to speak to Him. He tells believers that we may call on Him anytime and He will listen.

These toys and games are by far not the only worrisome toys on the market. Many video games, such as *Zork, Zeus, Quest* and *Dungeons of Death,* offer a considerable amount of violence and the occult. With these games, players take on the role of various characters and search for treasures, just as in the game of *Dungeons and Dragons.* To play these videos, children do not need to go to the nearest arcade. They can be used on most home computers. These games are laden with the occult, all of which are mentioned in the Bible as being abominations to the Lord.

It is no wonder children are more aggressive and display a tendency toward violent play. They have been *barbarized* by the constant influx of images depicting acts of aggression: from cartoons, commercials, movies and toys. It is up to us to reverse this trend and restore childhood innocence to playtime.

11

THE MIND TRAP

That wonderful world of "let's pretend" is being influenced today in a way that researchers never really considered a danger. Too much time spent in the imaginary world affects all ages, disorienting the way they view reality. **Psychologists have claimed, time and again, that when someone lives in the realm of fantasy for an extended length of time, the lines dividing reality and fantasy become distorted, fuzzy.**

In the last decade, this concept has been proven to be a real and increasing danger. The contributing force behind it for many youths has been *Dungeons and Dragons* and other fantasy role-playing games.

Dungeons and Dragons, commonly referred to as *D & D*, is a fantasy game in which each player assumes the identity of the character he creates. In this game, the "creature" that the player creates is based on the chance roll of the dice. *D & D* evolved from war games which were popular in the 1950s. In this game, instead of fighting on historical battlefields, battles are fought in the players' minds. The *Dungeon Master* (DM), often seen as a god, sets the stage in the fantasy world. The participants step into medieval personalities who journey through incredible adventures so far as their strengths and personalities will take them. Unlike other board games, there is no set ending to *D & D* and other fantasy role-playing games. Instead, the only limit to the game is the players' imaginations. For those with particularly vivid imaginations, the game can become an almost mystical experience, consuming, addictive, and potentially dangerous. In fact, there are many documented cases where a group of people played the same game for several years.

The object of *D & D*, designed for three or more players age ten and up, is to maneuver the characters through a maze of dungeons (tunnels) filled with monsters, magic, ambushes and adventures in search of treasures. Each character has six basic abilities, determined by the roll of the dice: strength, intelligence, wisdom, constitution, dexterity and charisma. Also, each character is equipped with special aids to survive the journey through the dungeons: magical weapons, potions, spells and magical trinkets, such as holy water, garlic and wolves-bane. They are also given more conventional weapons including daggers, hand axes, swords and battle axes. Each player can stay in the game so long as his character is not killed, thus, leaving open the possibility for the game to continue for years. However, the longer the game continues, the more likely the players will identify themselves with the character, causing the line between reality and fantasy to grow "fuzzy."[1]

Although Gary Gygax, creator of the *Dungeons and Dragons* game, contends the game is harmless and just a "fun" game, he does admit that the game can cause players to become too personally involved. "When you start playing out a fantasy, it can really eat up time and capture you totally," he told a reporter. "Most people can handle it, but there probably are exceptions. You can get very emotionally involved. I've got several characters I've nurtured through many tension-filled, terror-fraught *D & D* games, and I'd be really crushed if I lost one of them. They can become very much a part of you."[2]

The Society for Creative Anachronism is one example of a group of people who have become too involved in the game, to the point of obsession.[3] This nationwide, underground war-gaming club is comprised of members who wear medieval clothing—swords, steel helmets and all—and who adopt the lifestyle of their characters, even going so far as to wage live wars on fellow society members.

The war-gaming club is not alone in the examples of people who have become obsessed with fantasy role-playing games. Gygax himself says the makeup of *D & D* lends itself to an undisciplined overindulgence. "You have to pursue *D & D* with your whole soul if you're going to do well at it."[4] And when "pursuing the game with his whole soul," a player often has difficulty differentiating between the game and reality. This can be seen as one young man, who is an avid *D & D* player, recalls his ordeal to a reporter.[5] The young man was a sophomore, majoring in chemistry, at Michigan State University.

> He had been alone inside a musty fortress, lost in a maze of dank passageways that hid mortal dangers. He was armed only with a sword and a shield, scant protection from the grotesque monster that lurked there, waiting for him.
>
> Unable to escape, he had faced the creature, a huge, hairy, fire-breathing nightmare for which the young man had been no match in battle.
>
> "It killed me," he said. "Burned me to death."
>
> The young man's mood was serious. He said his hands were perspiring as he recounted the confrontation. He knew he was not dead. He knew that the fortress and the monster had not been real. But the memory of the fantasy he and several friends had created the night before was very real and it had shaken him badly.
>
> And he said he loved it.

"Fantasies, in and of themselves, serve a healthy function, like relieving boredom," says Michigan psychologist Dr. Jack McGaugh.[6] "Like any good thing, it can be overdone. What you think about, you become at the time." Another Michigan psychologist, Dr. Douglas Brown, believes the same. "Life for most people is boring. There's not much excitement.

We've run out of frontiers. The only frontiers we have left are in our minds. Testing yourself becomes the challenge."[7] He does offer one caution, however. "If a person isn't too well put together to begin with, it's not going to be good for him."

This author, however, does not agree.

> **STATEMENT:** "Fantasies, in and of themselves, serve a healthy function, like relieving boredom."
>
> **OBJECTION:** The more we fantasize on something, the more likely we are to bring that fantasy to reality through our actions. This can be either good or bad.
>
> **STATEMENT:** "The only frontier we have left is in our minds."
>
> **OBJECTION:** God gives us thoughts. The only true way we can expand our creative thinking is to establish and cultivate our relationship with God.

The game's creator Gary Gygax admits that *D & D* players are fervid followers. "They ARE dedicated. They get really caught up in it. But I've met some obsessed golfers and tennis players, too. *Dungeons and Dragons* is just a different kind of release."[8]

When Gygax and Dave Arneson, of Lake Geneva, Wisconsin, created the game in 1974, the biggest supporters of the game were college students. For them, *D & D* offered an escape from the intense demands of college academia.[9] As the game increased in popularity, post-college adults started playing. And eventually, the interest filtered down to the pre-teen age groups. Today, many secondary schools even offer "talented and gifted" students the opportunity to play *D & D* for credit during school hours. Some "classroom versions" of the game are even being produced. Many state-supported colleges are offering classes in *D & D;* however, there are also many who have cancelled them at the insistence of concerned parents and taxpayers. Still, college students are the game's strongest following.

"It (the game) allows you to work out frustrations and the doldrums of classes," one coed from Oakland University in Pontiac, Michigan, told a reporter. "You get away from everything. You can do anything you want to do, anything your wildest imagination will permit. But it's not dangerous. Sometimes I'm too busy creating dungeons and rolling up characters to do my homework, but I don't go out and live out my fantasies. Only nuts go into steam tunnels."[10]

According to Dieter H. Sturm, spokesman for the firm that markets *Dungeons and Dragons,* in 1983 there were three to four million *D & D* players in the United States.[11] There is also a strong *D & D* following in England and France.[12] According to the *Model Retailer* magazine, in 1980, *D & D* was equal in terms of national popularity with any board game, including *Monopoly.*[13] However, fantasy role-playing games still ranked behind electronic games in popularity.[14] Despite the fact that *Dungeons and Dragons* is equal in terms of popularity to any board game, *D & D* adherents do not play the game like any other. There are some who just "dabble," but there are also "real-lifers" who have basically lost all interest and motivation in the real world. These people spend all their waking hours in search of treasures at the expense of orcs and dragons. But the majority of players fall somewhere in between the two extremes, meeting once or twice a week, with a normal game lasting four to six hours.[15]

Despite the game's skyrocketing popularity, many people, both Christian and non-Christian, are expressing concerns over the harmful effects the game is having on today's youth. According to Dr. Gary North, author of *None Dare Call It Witchcraft,* said " . . . after years of study of the history of occultism, after having researched a book on the subject, and after having consulted with scholars in the field of historical research, I can say with confidence: these games are the most effective, most magnificently packaged, most profitably marketed, most thoroughly researched introduction to the occult in man's recorded history."[16]

Some may think the game is harmless, strictly fun, fantasy and entertainment. But, according to Rev. John A. Dekker, parents who allow their children to play with such games are opening their homes and children to the subtle introduction to the occult and malignant world of psychotherapy (mind alteration, values modification).[17] Dekker says these games are part of the increasing spread of the occult. After extensive research, *Christian Life Ministries* and other experts have concluded that *Dungeons and Dragons* is not a game. Instead, they claim it is a "teaching on demonology, witchcraft, voodoo, murder, rape, blasphemy, suicide, assassination, insanity, sex perversion, homosexuality, prostitution, Satan worship, gambling, Jungian psychology, barbarism, cannibalism, sadism, desecration, demon summoning, necromantics, and divination."[18] In fact, these are all behaviors and practices that God forbids in the Old and New Testaments.

> *When thou art come into the land which the Lord thy God giveth thee, thou shalt not learn to do after the abominations of those nations.*
>
> *There shall not be found among you any one that maketh his son or daughter to pass through the fire, or that useth divination, or an observer of times, or an enchanter, or a witch,*
>
> *Or a charmer, or a consulter with familiar spirits, or a wizard, or a necromancer.*
>
> *For all that do these things are an abomination unto the Lord: and because of these abominations the Lord thy God doth drive them out from before thee.*[19]

There are many other references to God speaking about *D & D* terms in the Bible. Some of the references include: Exodus 20:3-6, 22:18, and 23:13; Isaiah 8:19-20 and 47:9-13; I Corinthians 10:14, 20-22; and Revelation 22:14-15. Galatians 5:19-21 also talks about terms and practices that *D & D* puts to use in a fantasy role-playing way:

> *Now the deeds of the flesh are plain: fornication, impurity, licentiousness, idolatry, sorcery, enmity, strife, jealousy, anger, selfishness, dissension, party spirit, envy, drunkenness, carousing, and the like. I warn you, as I warned you before, that those who do such things shall not inherit the kingdom of God.* (RSV)

Although *D & D* is not a religion per se, it does teach religious principles and familiarize players with terms and rituals of occult forms of religion. A few years ago, the game came under fire when many groups claimed the game was "anti-religious, filled with pictures and symbols you could find in any basic witchcraft book." But *Gygax* is quick to defend his demons: "The game is neither good nor evil. It is simply a good time, and for some students, a tool to learn." As for the witchcraft found in the book: "I made up all the spells out of my head. How can anyone take them seriously? The ingredient in one of the spells is 'legumes.'"[20]

Despite Gygax's denial that the game is occult, there are many references to traditional Christian terms, such as atonement, deity, faith, fasting, resurrection, God, prayer and Divine Ascension, that are treated in a blasphemous manner in the players' handbooks and various other D & D guide books.

According to the *American College Encyclopedic Dictionary*, blasphemy is the "impious utterance or action concerning God or sacred things; the crime of assuming to oneself the rights or qualities of God; and the irreverent behavior toward anything held sacred."

Some examples of blasphemy are found in quotes taken from the more than 20 books that teach how to play *Dungeons and Dragons*:

Concerning "Deities" and "Gods"

"This game lets all your fantasies come true. This is a world where monsters, dragons, good and evil; high priests, fierce demons; and even the gods themselves may enter your character's life."[21]

On other sections the gods are referred to as "deity:"

(1) "It is well known by all experienced players . . . spells bestowed upon them by their respective deities."[22]

(2) "Each cleric must have his or her own deity.[23]

(3) "The deity (you the DM 'Dungeon Master') will point out all the transgressions. . . . "[24]

"Serving a deity is a significant part of D & D, and all player characters should have a patron god. Alignment assumes its full importance when tied to the worship of a deity."[25]

"Changing alignment: Whether or not the character actively professes some deity, he or she will have an alignment and serve one or more deities of this general alignment indirectly or unbeknownst to the character."[26]

Concerning Prayer and Fasting

"Clerical spells . . . are bestowed by the gods, so that the cleric need but pray for a few hours. . . . "[27]

"Cleric desires third through fifth level spells, the minions (angels, demigods, or whatever) will be likely to require the cleric to spend two to eight days in prayer, fasting, and contemplation of his or her transgressions, making whatever sacrifices and atonement are necessary . . . Spell recovery . . . requires about the same period of time. In order to pray and meditate. . . . "[28]

Concerning Magic and Spells

"Swords and sorcery best describe what this game is all about . . . so mind unleashing, that it comes near reality."[29]

"Most spells have a verbal component and so must be uttered."[30]

"The spell caster should be required to show you what form of protective inscription he or she has used when the spell is cast." The three forms mentioned are: Pictures of a magic circle, pentagram, and thaumaturgic triangle."[31] According to experts in the occult, these symbols are commonly used in witchcraft and Satanic worship.

Concerning Clerics

"Another important attribute of the cleric is the ability to turn away (or actually command into service) the undead and less powerful demons and devils."[32]

Concerning Death

"Resurrection" is referred to as "the revival of a character after its death, by magical means."[33]

Concerning Satanism

"Elric (hero)"—the sign being given by his left hand (which is called the Goat Head sign) means "Satan is Lord" to all Satan worshippers.[34]

The word "demon" appears 106 times in pages 16-19 of the *Monster Manual.* And the player has been told to trust four of these demons as (lesser gods) on page 105, paragraph 5, of the *Deities and Demigods* book.

The word "devil" appears 94 times and the word "hell" appears 25 times in pages 20-23 of the *Monster Manual.*

Concerning Defilement

In the following excerpt from page 115 of the *Players Handbook,* bless and curse, and unholy and holy are treated as equals.

"Defilement of Fonts: If any non-believer blesses/curses an unholy/holy font, or uses less refined means such as excreting wastes into a font or basin, the whole is absolutely desecrated, defiled, and unfit . . . Note that either method of defilement requires actual contact with the font and its vessel. Any blessing or cursing from a distance will be absolutely ineffectual and wasted."

The above practices that the game employs and forces the players to do likewise are indeed the exact practices that God forbids in the Bible. Still many Christians say, "I'm a Christian, and I play *D & D.*" And others contend that the game is just fantasy, that they would never do these things in real life. In the *New Testament,* Christ teaches that fantasy can be evil. *"But I say unto you, That whosoever looketh on a woman to lust after her hath committed adultery with her already in his heart."*[35] With this verse,

Christ establishes that sin can exist in the heart and mind, even though the acts themselves may never be committed. Thus, according to God's plan, those fantasizing about these occult practices are just as guilty as if they had performed the acts.

Because of the very nature of the "occult," many people have difficulty in seeing that *Dungeons and Dragons* does in fact deal with the occult and helps spur interest in the occult. A former dungeon master, who is now attending *Christian Life Ministries,* says this about the game: "One definition of occult is hidden, concealed. I played *D & D* for three years, became interested in tarot cards and still did not realize that I was dealing with occult practices. Therefore I have nothing against anyone who plays *D & D,* but I am critical of *D & D* itself."[36]

In 1981, the game was banned by the Cordova Park Board because of the game's religious/occult overtones. George Marsh, a member of the board, explained why he voted to ban the game in a letter to the editor of a Sacramento daily newspaper: "The Supreme Court has already barred religious activity from public facilities. *Dungeons and Dragons* is clearly religious in content."[37]

Still, the occult overtones are not the only concern that Christians have regarding the game. The time consumption required by the game and the fact that this could lead to overidentification with the characters is another real hazard.

Lee Gold, publisher of *Alarums and Excursions,* describes how he feels about the game: "Evil is disgusting, and you'd better be vivid about it. I've seen ghouls eat sweet-and-sour babies. But going into all that . . . it's just silly. Ripping off genitals. Girdles of sex change. It's immature. It's dull, but not dangerous. The stuff that makes me nervous is overidentification with characters. I've seen people have fits, yell for 15 minutes, and hurl dice at a grand piano when their character dies."[38]

Unlike *Monopoly* and other board games, *Dungeons and Dragons* becomes a compulsive force in the lives of those who play it. *D & D* requires each player to make philosophical, religious and moral decisions, whereas ordinary board games do not. Eventually, the more a player participates in the game, the more he chooses to remain in the fantasy world, the harder it will be for him to accept his responsibilities in the real world.

Consider the following story about John, a 16-year-old sophomore at a Southern California college.[39]

> He sits in his small dorm room, $900 worth of handpainted miniatures covering the bed.
>
> "Ever since I was 10, I've wanted to drop out of this world. There are so many flaws. A lot of things are unfair. When I'm in my own world, I control my own world order. I can picture it all. The groves and trees. The beauty. I can hear the wind. The world isn't like that. My beliefs, morals, sense of right and wrong are much stronger since playing *D & D*," he says.
>
> But, in comparison, the real world becomes less tenable.
>
> "It's hazardous. Your vocabulary, your mental quickness increases, but school seems increasingly boring and droll. Your grades drop. The more time you spend in your fantasy world, the more you want to walk away from the burdensome decisions of life.
>
> "The more I play *D & D*, the more I want to get away from this world. The whole thing is getting very bad."

We must recognize the dangers of our children spending so much time playing this game. It often leads to a distortion of reality, as well as filling the child's mind with images of the occult. The Word reminds us that we should " . . . *be careful how you walk, not as unwise men, but as wise, making the most of your time, because the days are evil.*"[40]

Lastly, another prime concern of most Christians is the harm caused by fantasy role-playing itself. It is true that engaging in fantasy is beneficial to child development—so long as the fantasy is not based on images that will corrupt the child's thinking. Remember, these images do not cause a direct effect. No, the corruption occurs slowly, just a little at a time, over a period of years. This is the danger of *subtle deception.*

Fantasy role-playing is "a subtle (sugar-coated) form of psycho-drama adapted to Humanistic designs for sensitivity training and values modification." In fact, role-playing is the "first-step form of psychotherapy that can destroy what Humanists call the "God syndrome."[41] The "God syndrome" is what Humanists refer to as "belief in God." Thus, in other words, "fantasy role-playing is the first step toward subtly introducing the child to reject the religious training of church and home."[42]

Psychodramatic techniques, which are the root of role-playing, were introduced by Dr. Jacob L. Moreno, a contemporary of Sigmund Freud, in the early 1900s. Moreno wanted to "develop a positive religion." In his 1932 book, *Who Shall Survive,* Moreno wrote that through psychodrama (role-playing), "we will destroy the God syndrome." Moreno believed that if you can "play a role," for instance the role of God, "and develop that role and stop its playing at will, you will begin to learn how not to be possessed of that role. The only way to get rid of the God syndrome is to act it out."[43] This "positive religion" that Moreno envisioned is all part of Humanism—a religion that makes man all-powerful. It is these very beliefs that are incorporated in *Dungeons and Dragons.* In the players' minds, they create characters who are all-powerful, capable of controlling demons and other monsters.

We must realize that when the burdens of life get too heavy, we do not have to turn to fantasy, because Jesus has already provided an escape:

Even though I walk through the valley of the shadow of death, I fear no evil; for thou art with me; thy rod and thy staff, they comfort me.

Thou preparest a table before me in the presence of my enemies; thou annointest my head with oil, my cup overflows.

Surely goodness and mercy shall follow me all the days of my life; and I shall dwell in the house of the Lord for ever.[44]

12

FROM SILVER SCREEN TO TOY BOX

In addition to marketing products in conjunction with children's television programming, toy industries realize that "big bucks" also can be made in designing toys to correspond with blockbuster movies. In a small way, toy companies have always designed toys to correspond with popular movies, but, not to the extent and fervor seen today.

It all began in 1977 with a blast into hyperspace—the debut of George Lucas' film, *Star Wars*. In the nine years since, retail sales of *Star Wars* licensed products have reached $2.5 billion. And this is a conservative estimate, Sid Ganis, senior vice president of marketing for Lucasfilm Ltd., said in a special advertising supplement to the February 1986 edition of *Toy and Hobby World*.[1] Since that time, movies have brought us every alien imaginable—and unimaginable. From the *Star Wars* trilogy, we have seen *Droids*, those robots known as *C-3PO* and *R2-D2*; *Ewoks*, furry little "teddy bears" that live in the forest; *Yoda*, an elf-like creature known as the *Zen Master*; and *Darth Vader*, a semi-human master of evil. The list does not stop here. Stephen Spielberg's *Extra-Terrestrial* introduced us to the fetus-like-looking *E.T.*, and his movie *Gremlins* starred furry, mischievous creatures known as *Mogwai*, or *Gremlins*. The 1984 film, *Ghostbusters*, produced by Columbia Pictures, did not introduce any aliens. Instead, it presented ghosts, those creatures that are found in everyone's imagination. The movie focused on the efforts of three men who made a living from exterminating ghosts. Whatever, be they aliens or ghosts, America has "adopted" these creatures and taken them to heart. Most have opened their pocketbooks and homes to them. In fact, Americans have spent hundreds of millions of dollars on these toys, designed after creatures which were given life on the silver screens.

These odd-looking creatures have become "classics" for the moviegoer. Toy companies have capitalized on America's love affair with them by selling licenses to all key merchandise areas: apparel/accessories, food products, home textiles, housewares, publishing and music, stationery and gifts, toys, and a host of juvenile products. In this affluent society, children can wear their favorite "alien" to bed and even drink milk while looking at his face on the glass.

Since the movie premier in 1977, *Star Wars*-related products have been a major part of Kenner toy line. "The longevity of the *Star Wars* franchise has been unprecedented in the toy industry, especially in terms of a toy line derived from a movie license," said Bill Bracy, senior vice president of marketing for Kenner.[2] Kenner keeps pace with the interest by introducing new toys to correspond with every *Star Wars* sequel, as well as the new Saturday morning cartoons, *The Ewoks and Droids Adventure Hour.* "We are excited to plan for the merchandising success that will come from a weekly reinforcement of the fantasy through Saturday morning programming. The toys can extend the experience and fun the child has with the *Ewoks* and *Droids* TV series," Bracy continued.[3] Some of the toys designed to correspond with the cartoons include new action figures, plush toys, vehicles, play sets, collectors' cases and other accessories.

Toy companies do not just introduce new toys to correspond with new shows. They also mount full-scale promotional and advertising campaigns. One promotion which Kenner is planning for this year involves a mail-in offer for a free *Droid* companion with three proofs-of-purchase of the action figures. Regretfully, children are bombarded with this sort of thing. They see these characters in movies, on Saturday morning cartoons and in toy stores. It is no wonder that the constant influx of these movie characters into the media is causing a considerable amount of peer pressure for children to buy these toys.

However, Lucasfilm Ltd. spokesmen say the demand for *Star Wars* toys and other toys that have originated from Lucas' films is because of the quality of the movies themselves—not because of high-pressured sales pitches.[4] Lucasfilm Ltd. maintains they do not create toys to push the movies and cartoons. They claim it is the enduring popularity of these characters, such as *R2-D2*, *C-3PO* and *Ewoks*, that has spurred the spectacularly successful licensing division at Lucasfilm Ltd. "It is Lucasfilm's high caliber, innovative entertainment products, such as its theatrical releases, live-action television films and animated television shows, that 'drive the licensing and produce the consumer demand,'" said Maggie Young, vice president of merchandise licensing at Lucasfilm Ltd.[5] "The licensing division's very real goal is to enhance the final entertainment product. Without the wonderful entertainment created by Lucasfilm, licensing would not be successful," she continued. Ganis, senior vice president of marketing for Lucasfilm, echoes Young's statements. "Licensing has been a great business for us over the years, but it has never been our motivating factor. Look at our logo—Lucasfilm. It states unequivocally that we are, first and foremost, a film company. Our primary purpose at Lucasfilm is to entertain kids of all ages," he said.[6]

Whatever the reasons for releasing toys to correspond with movie premiers, the practice has resulted in billions of dollars in sales, as well as drawing much criticism. Parents, child psychologists, clergy and even government agencies have expressed concern over the exploitation of children in order to sell products. The young child, who is easily persuaded, will hound his parents relentlessly to buy his favorite cartoon character. Often, the parents are unwilling. They are unwilling for various reasons. Perhaps, it is a moral concern, or perhaps the parent just does not think the toy is suitable for the child. Whatever the reasons, most parents give in. As a result, the child is happy—he has the toy. But, the parents must worry about the negative effects the toy will have on the child.

"What negative effects? The movies are just science fiction, fantasy. They are harmless." Or so you think. These *harmless* movies are like the "cute and innocent" toys discussed in an earlier chapter. The movies appear to be only a "cute journey into fantasy." Under that innocent-looking facade, however, lie a considerable amount of occult symbolisms. Like the movies from whence they came, the toys are laden with the occult, but on a more subtle level. No matter how "cute" these toys appear, parents should not let their children play with them.

Children are a special gift from God which should be cherished. *Lo, sons are a heritage from the Lord, the fruit of the womb a reward.*[7] The Lord gives further instructions to parents in Deuteronomy 6:4-7.

> Hear, O Israel: The Lord our God is one Lord; and you shall love the Lord your God with all your heart, and with all your soul, and with all your might. And these words which I command you this day shall be on your heart; and you shall teach them diligently to your children, and you shall talk of them when you sit in your house, and when you walk by the way, and when you lie down, and when you rise. (RSV)

I am not saying that parents refrain from censoring their children's television and movie viewing. I am saying, however, parents are not always aware of the dangers that may be lurking in certain films. Many parents do censor their children's viewing so that television shows and movies portraying too much sex and violence are prohibited. But what about the movies billed as "good family entertainment"? Many parents do not give these movies a second thought—after all, they say, it is "family entertainment."

Consider this movie scene: a husband and wife are crushed to death by a snowplow, the victims of a deliberate act of aggression. By most standards, this scene would be considered extremely violent and unsuitable for children. However, when it was shown, moviegoers laughed hilariously. Why? Were they all sadistic? No. The audience laughed because it was the *Gremlins* who crushed the man and woman in the *Gremlins* movie. In fact, the entire *Gremlins* movie was filled with violence—*Gremlins* killing and viciously attacking people—with rebellion and lawlessness. Why was the movie regarded as funny and acceptable for children? Because the creatures' shocking, evil behavior was masked with a cloak of humor. It was OK, acceptable. It seems unGodly behavior and influences are acceptable when presented in the guise of humor.[8]

It is these subtleties of which parents must be aware. Parents must not be enamored by the cute, outward appearance of these "aliens." Instead, they should pay attention to the "magic" and other occult practices with which these characters are associated. Children also should be taught these toy characters are not in accordance with God's teachings. Previously we spoke about *subtle deception*. It is this same *subtle deception* which makes it possible for these "cute aliens" to spur a subliminal interest in the occult. Satan deceives us with the "alien's" cute appearance, working his evil influences into a child's subconscious. As the child grows older, so does his interest in the occult—until it becomes a fascination and then an obsession. It is imperative to follow the directions set forth in Scripture: *Train up a child in the way he should go, and when he is old he will not depart from it.*[9]

Parents often question, "If a movie is advertised for children, how can I tell that it won't have occult symbolisms?" Unfortunately, it is almost impossible to know this in advance of viewing the movie. This dilemma is becoming more difficult for parents since film makers are producing darker, more violent films aimed, at least partly, at a pre-teen audience.[10] As a result, there is growing concern among parents and child development experts about what youngsters are actually seeing when they go to movies. Movies released in the last two years, many of which have spawned successful toy lines, have caused special concerns for critics and child psychologists. Some of the eyebrow-raising movie scenes included: the violence and child enslavement of *Indiana Jones and the Temple of Doom;* smirky cruelty of the *Gremlins;* casual attitude for killing in *Star Trek III: The Search for Spock;* the explosive violence of *Firestarter;* the unrelenting pace and brutality of *Return of the Jedi;* and the otherworldly creatures in *The Neverending Story.*[11] In response to the concerns, industry executives have ratified a new ratings system to differentiate between films for those under and over 13 years old.

This new ratings system has upset others who say today's movies are no "darker" to young viewers than the *Wicked Witch of the West* and her monkey henchmen in *The Wizard of Oz.* Jim Henson, creator of the *Muppets,* disagrees. "I think the darker side of things is coming into fantasy films. There are a couple of films which have stronger scenes than I think you would have seen even two or three years ago."[12]

Most critics will say, however, they do not find fault only with the graphic violence in these newly-released films. Their greatest concern is with the intensity of the films. "The new movies, like the *Star Wars* films, are authoritarian," according to child psychologist Bruno Bettelheim. Bettelheim refers to the "breakneck pace and emphatic editing that can be overpowering for young children."[13] Most child experts do not deny that children's films and literature always have contained material that some parents and children found disturbing. Even *Snow White, Dumbo* and *The Wizard of Oz* have had some frightening elements. The difference between these and more recent films does not lie in the content, but in the way in which the story is told. "The *Disney* films presented a world in which there was a moral order. And there was a sweetness in the way they told their stories that is several levels removed from the vivid realism of *Indiana Jones*," said Neil Postman.[14] Postman is an expert of the effect of the media on children and he is the author of *The Disappearance of Childhood.*

When did all these changes take place? At one time, many "G-rated" movies were produced. Today, however, these movies are hard to find. Do film makers think there is no market in producing films that depict gentleness and goodness, which would be perfect for young viewers? Most experts say the changes began with the summer blockbuster *Jaws* several years back. Experts say the film industry learned that it was not necessary to target a film for either children or parents—they could have both.

"Older moviegoers feel embarrassed when they see a movie made just for children," Henson said. "So film makers have tried to include things that would appeal to (adults) as well. When the heart is pulled out in *Indiana Jones,* you know you're no longer watching a kiddie movie."[15] Postman aggrees that the desire to attract both young and older viewers has darkened the content of children's films. "In the pursuit of an ever-larger audience, film makers have escalated the amount of brutality and terror in their films," he said.[16]

As a result of these changes in the movie industry, the characters being produced in the films also have undergone changes. Today, popular characters are ghosts or aliens from outerspace. These characters then capture the hearts of moviegoers everywhere.

It is very innocent—until we realize the movies are filled with the occult and these "ever popular characters" are really contradictory to God's teachings. For this reason, I have decided to include a chapter in this book about toys that have been derived from recent blockbuster movies, which have set unprecedented attendance records. In fact, one of the biggest grossing movies ever made has been *Rambo*. This movie is extremely violent; yet, it draws crowds. I recently heard a statistic that one out of every four movie tickets sold in 1986 has been for the two movies Sylvester Stallone is in and the two movies Stephen Spielberg produced. This includes every ticket bought in every theater. One out of every four tickets sold will be for one of those four movies. Because of this ever-increasing popularity of movies, it is important to discuss the effects movies are having on children, especially when linked to corresponding toys.

THE SILVER SCREEN

The top money-making films of today focus on preternatural manifestations of the kingdom of darkness. First there was *Rosemary's Baby, The Exorcist, Omen* and *Poltergeist*. Then came a variety of others designed for children: *Star Wars* trilogy, *E.T., Ghostbusters* and *Gremlins*. With the continual bombardment of these movies, Americans have become desensitized in discerning what is evil. The influence of preternatural manifestations is not limited to the silver screen. With the advent of television, occult shows also became popular: *Bewitched, I Dream of*

Jeannie, The Twilight Zone and *Dark Shadows.* Next came shows such as *Batman* and *Wonderwoman,* which featured humans displaying preternatural strengths and powers. No wonder Saturday morning cartoons have followed suit. The shows no longer contain subtle innuendoes of occult power; instead, they portray blatant demonstrations of witchcraft, sorcery and occult rituals. All of which are detested by God in Deuteronomy 18:10-14.

Regardless of the anti-Christian content of these movies, Americans are flocking to see them. Through these movies, Satan gets a hold of our hearts and minds. Satan is methodically teaching our youth that demons are real, but cute, friendly and helpful. Unknowingly, youngsters will ally themselves with demons and become willing disciples and slaves of Satan. In fact, Americans are glorifying Satan and promoting his war against the church by going to see movies that feature occult philosophies and phenomena and by buying children toys and T-shirts, portraying devilish human mutations and creatures that are featured in the movies.[17]

Webster's Dictionary defines "demon" as a "devil; evil spirit; a person or thing regarded as evil, cruel, etc." Does this creature sound like anything that would be "cute, friendly and helpful"? It does not sound like the demons of which Jesus spoke. *The thief comes only to steal and kill and destroy; I came that they may have life, and have it abundantly.*[18]

The practice of allying oneself to Satan's influences is not new. It dates back to Biblical times when the Psalmist wrote of Israelites who allied themselves with the unGodly beliefs and activities of Canaanites.

> *They did not destroy the peoples, as the Lord commanded them, but they mingled with the nations and learned to do as they did.*
> *They served their idols, which became a snare to them.*
> *They sacrificed their sons and their daughters to the demons;*

> they poured out innocent blood, the blood of their sons and daughters, whom they sacrificed to the idols of Canaan; and the land was polluted with blood.
>
> Thus they became unclean by their acts, and played the harlot in their doings.
>
> Then the anger of the Lord was kindled against his people, and he abhorred his heritage;
>
> he gave them into the hand of the nations, so that those who hated them ruled over them.[19]

Can these same behaviors be compared with today's parents? If we allow our children to be exposed constantly to gremlins, ghosts, aliens, wizards, witches, enchanters and psychics, knowing that they are an abomination to God, are we not guilty of sacrificing our children to demons as the Israelites did?[20]

STAR WARS

For the sake of simplicity, the three *Star Wars* films: *Star Wars, The Empire Strikes Back* and *Return of the Jedi*, will be considered as one unit. The two sequels, as well as the Saturday morning cartoons, *The Ewoks and Droids Adventure Hour,* were all given birth from the popularity of the original *Star Wars* film. Although the story lines are somewhat different in each of the shows, the basic occult practices and phenomena are the same.

The *Star Wars* trilogy introduced thousands of Americans to the pagan religion of *Zen Buddhism* through the character *Yoda,* the little elf-like creature known as *Zen Master. Yoda* taught *Luke Skywalker,* a type of *Zen Buddhist monk,* about the ever-present *Force.* It may be interesting to note that the *Force* is a word used by witches down through the ages to describe the power they receive from Satan. It is this energy source which given impetus to the battle between *Darth Vader* and *Luke Skywalker.*

The *Force* is viewed as a deity that possesses both good and evil sides. *Obi-Wan Kenobi* describes it as "a powerful energy field created by all living things who both take from it and give to it. This energy can be tapped by those who are trained to do so. The *Force* requires faith (not everyone believes it exists), but it does not have a personality. It 'runs strong' in certain people, but it does not have a will of its own—it acts when a person's will is exerted upon it."[21]

The *Force* can be used for good or evil, depending upon the desire of the person who, through mind control, manipulates it. In the movies, *Yoda* teaches *Luke* to reach down inside himself to utilize the power inherent to his mind and direct the *Force* for the purpose of "good." This philosophy is pure *Zen Buddhism*. What better *god* could fallen man desire than one that he can command and control at will?

Yoda does, however, teach *Luke* about the dangers of following the dark side of the *Force*. *Yoda* tells *Luke* that the dark side is seductive and one must constantly guard against its temptations. "Beware of anger, fear and aggression, the dark side are they," *Yoda* tells *Luke* in *Return of the Jedi*. "Once you start down the dark path, forever will it dominate your destiny." Although this statement does have similarities with Jesus' teachings, it also contains elements of other religions: *Taoism, Islam* and *Judaism*. In fact, the idea of identifying God as a "force of nature," is pantheistic and dualistic.[22] Both of which are against God's teachings.

Many claim the *Star Wars* trilogy should not be considered occult because it talks about good versus evil. It demonstrates that following the "good side" might not always be easy, but it is the best way, in the end. Regardless, it is occult. Any practice that does not have glorifying God as its root, but glorifies Satan or other gods, is occult. *Yoda* does not talk about following Jesus Christ. Instead, he urges *Luke* to rely on himself and use the power inherent to his mind to do "good." This is a contradiction to God's teachings. This makes *Luke* an equal to God. He is taught to handle situations on his own, not needing God's assistance.

Occult practices and symbolisms are not limited to *Yoda's Zen Buddhistic* teachings. *Luke* also uses "magic," which is one of the practices listed in Deuteronomy as an abomination to the Lord. In various scenes, *Luke* uses the *Force* to levitate objects. Also, George Lucas, executive producer of the trilogy, admits to being strongly influenced by Carlos Castaneda's *Tales of Powers*. The book chronicles the story of Don Juan, a Mexican Indian sorcerer, who speaks of a life force. Another interesting point concerns *Darth Vader, Luke's* real father who followed the *Force's* path of evil. *Darth Vader* wears a black mask which covers his face, making him appear almost machine-like. Centuries ago, in the times of Norsemen, the Norsemen made huge wooden masks to represent gods in their myths. In the *Star Wars* trilogy, *Darth Vader* shows strong similarities to the Norsemen's representation of their god *Oden*. Myths are based on characters who are said to possess God-like qualities and powers. In ancient times, people worshipped these gods, as the Israelites worshipped idols. These symbolisms, which have root in mythology, add to the occult nature of the films.

There are still those, however, who insist the movie has Christian ideals flowing through it. That may be true. Then, the danger here is the "incompleteness of the gospel." Some of the ideals presented could lead people to stray from the truth of the gospel. The elements that make Christianity a unique faith is the belief in the redemption of man through the death of Jesus Christ and his resurrection.[23] This belief is not seen in the *Jedi religion,* not even in an allegorical sense. In *Return of the Jedi, Darth Vader's* salvation does not come through his repentance, but through the vanquishing of the evil *Emperor*.[24] This "incompleteness of the gospel" causes concern among many Christians.

Many are afraid teenagers will develop false notions about religion or adopt false doctrine as a result of the *Star Wars* influence. Even George Lucas believes films have an impact on how society operates. He says films have taken over the power of teaching our youth that once was held by the church. "Film and other visual entertainment are a pervasively important part of our culture, an extremely significant influence on the way our society operates. People in the film industry don't want to accept the responsibility that they had a hand in the way the world is loused up. But, for better or for worse, the influence of the church, which used to be all powerful, has been usurped by film. Films and television tell us the way we conduct our lives, what is right and wrong. When Burt Reynolds is drunk on beer in *Hooper* and racing cops in his rocket car, that reinforces the recklessness of the kids who've been drawn to the movie in the first place and are probably sitting in the theater drinking beer."[25]

However, Lucas denies all of the religious inferences that Christians have drawn from his films. "I was trying to say in a very simple way, knowing that the film was made for a young audience, that there is a God and there is both a good side and a bad side. You have a choice between them, but the world works better if you're on the good side. It's that simple."[26]

Whatever message he intended to present, there is no denying that occult practices and symbolisms are used throughout the trilogy as well as in Saturday morning cartoons. These shows are having a tremendous influence on our youth. They see *Yoda* as a "cute" being who helps *Luke* do good. They do not, at least consciously, see the occult philosophies that *Yoda* is teaching. Nevertheless, Satan has made his statement.

When we buy our children toys that are associated with the *Star Wars* saga, we are reinforcing the acceptability of these teachings. When children play with toys that are based on cartoons, they re-enact what they have seen the characters do on television. The same is true with movies. Many children have been seen pretending to be *Luke Skywalker* and using the *Force* to fight evil. They have been observed on playgrounds pointing plastic imitations of *Luke's lightsabers* at their friends and saying, "May the *Force* be with you."

Do we really want children to think that they can rely on their own powers to fight evil?

Although *Yoda* and the *Force* are indeed occult images presented in the *Star Wars* saga, they are not the only creatures that have been created from the trilogy. Since the first movie premiered in 1977, *Ewoks* and *Droids* also have been created. Like the "beloved" *Yoda*, these creatures have captured the hearts of Americans. A movie has been made starring *Ewoks,* and an hour-long Saturday morning cartoon was created in 1985 starring *Ewoks* and *Droids,* which reaches 19.6 million viewers each week. These creatures also have spawned a successful and quite extensive toy line.

Ewoks employ magic in their shows. On one cartoon episode, the emblem of *Zen Buddhism* appeared from nowhere and hung in the sky like a moon. In another episode, a witch tried to burn down the forest where the *Ewoks* live by casting a spell on the good fairies, making them carry fire. During the fire, the *Ewok's soul trees,* which are planted whenever an *Ewok* is born, cried out telepathically to the *Ewoks*. This is an inference to pagan religions which believe that there are spirits in every living thing.

Although I have not seen occult symbolisms in the *Droids* cartoon, parents should use their own discretion because of the show's origin. Another objection I have to these cartoons is the use of rock music to set the tempo for the show. Stewart Copeland of the British rock group *The Police* wrote the music for the *Droids; Taj Mahal* wrote the music for the *Ewoks*.

By buying toys and other merchandise corresponding to movies and cartoons, we are promoting Satan's work of *subtle deception*.

E.T.

To understand *E.T.* the toy, we must look at *E.T.* the movie. The *Extra-Terrestrial (E.T.)*, which has become a legend for movie fans, grossed $313 million in 1982. At first, the movie appears to be just another cute science fiction movie. But, occult symbolisms are there, only camouflaged.

The movie begins with a group of young boys playing *Dungeons and Dragons,* a game laden with the occult. In fact, page 7 of the *D & D Handbook* says, "Swords and Sorcery best describe what this game is all about. . . . " Later that night during dinner, Elliot, the young star of the movie, calls his brother "penis breath" during an argument. Does the mother get mad? No, she just laughs. Is this the example we want to set for our children? Do we want them to think that they can say nasty things to their siblings without fear of reprimand from their parents? Remember, children are impressionable. Their values and ideals must be molded. If parents do not take the time to do so, their children eventually will learn distorted beliefs and values from television and movies.

As the movie continues, the use of occult symbolisms increases. After *E.T.* arrives at Elliot's house, he and Elliot become joined by a psychic link of mental telepathy. The two even levitate together above the trees while riding Elliot's bicycle. Mental telepathy and levitation are common practices of mediums. In Deuteronomy 18:9-12, God specifically prohibits anyone from practicing as a medium because it is "detestable" to the Lord. In Galatians 5:19-21, Paul warns that anyone practicing such shall not inherit the kingdom of God.

Toward the end of the movie, *E.T.* becomes very sick and dies. He then resurrects himself and ascends in his spaceship back to his planet. This scene is similar to the resurrection of Christ and his ascension into heaven. The difference is that Jesus is God; whereas, *E.T.* is a demonic-looking alien who is not God. Throughout the movie, *E.T.* is portrayed as having God-like powers.

Lastly, throughout the movie, adults were against *E.T.*, so the children hid *E.T.* to keep him safe from these adults. The subtle thought created here is that "humans are inferior to aliens." In every science fiction "alien" movie, television show and video game, aliens are always portrayed as superior to humans. But, Genesis 1:26-27 states, *Then God said, "Let us make man in our image, after our likeness; and let them have dominion over the fish of the sea, and over the birds of the air, and over the cattle, and over all the earth, and over every creeping thing that creeps upon the earth." So God created man in his own image, in the image of God he created them; male and female he created them* (RSV). In light of this Scripture, there is no room for superior beings.

As far as the toy itself is concerned, there is not much to say. The movie, like other cartoons and movies, fills the children with images laden with the occult. The child then visualizes these occult practices while playing. Over time, the child will have more of a foundation in the occult than he will have in God's teachings.

GREMLINS

The furry, mischievous *Gremlins* created a stir in the toy market similar to that created by *E.T.* and characters from the *Star Wars* saga. These creatures are seen everywhere—on glasses, toys, T-shirts; there is even a *Gremlins* cereal for children.

Gremlins, executive produced by Stephen Spielberg, is about Billy Peltzer, a young man who dreams of becoming a hero. His inventor father gives Billy a furry creature—a *Mogwai*—as a Christmas present. Billy names the creature *Gizmo.* But in caring for *Gizmo,* Billy breaks some of the rules concerning *Mogwai* care that his father told him never to forget. One of the rules states that a *Mogwai* should never get wet. But Billy inadvertantly gets water on *Gizmo.* As a result, the *Mogwai* spawns five other *Mogwai.* Although these other five creatures look like *Gizmo,* they are drawn to do mischievous pranks. After a strange chain of events, sparked by breaking more Mogwai rules, the creatures develop into nasty *gremlins,* who are led by *Stripe,* the most malicious *gremlin.* The *gremlins* wreak havoc, spreading a path of destruction, chaos and death. Billy becomes a hero as he and *Gizmo* clash with the *gremlins* and eventually defeat them. *Stripe* is destroyed. But, *Gizmo* still exists. Eventually, *Gizmo's* original owner, an elderly storekeeper who sells occult items, takes him back.

Gremlins are legendary creatures who are known to be mischievous and have a good time causing havoc and generally making life difficult. In World War II, the term became popular. According to movie producers, *Gremlins* were accused of getting into machinery, especially airplaines, and fouling them up. There have been many theories for the origin of *gremlins.* Among these include: a goblin which came out of Fremlin's beer bottles; an ill-humored little fellow. Another source traces the word *gremlin* to the Old English word gemian, meaning to vex. Whatever theory you want to believe, *gremlins* are similar to the meaning of demon given in *Webster's Dictionary*—a devil; evil spirit; a person or thing regarded as evil, cruel, etc.[27]

This being the case, it would be logical to assume that it

would not be pleasing to God for His children to be playing with such toys. When a child plays with these toys, the images of the occult, presented in the movie, are strengthened in his mind.

However, images of Satanism and the occult are not limited to the legends and appearance of these creatures. The rules that *Gremlins* owners must follow also are laden with occult images. These rules are written on every box containing a *Gremlin:*

WARNING!

You must obey all *Mogwai* rules! Keep them away from water. Don't ever get them wet. Keep them out of light. They hate bright light . . . It will kill them. But the most important thing, the thing you must never forget, no matter how much they cry, no matter how much they beg, never, NEVER, feed them after midnight!

Because these devilish-looking creatures are not promoting the kingdom of God, the rules are obvious. Jesus says He is the Living Water and the Light of the World. It is also true that demons run away when faced with the power of Jesus. Jesus is the Living Water, and when we drink from the River of Life, we thirst no more. Therefore, any creature promoting the work of Satan would be certain to stay away from water. The same is true with light. Jesus is the Light of the World. He brings to light those things hidden in darkness. His Light of goodness and truth will indeed kill them.[28]

When the rule states that the creatures should not be fed past midnight, it implies that these creatures are alive. That extends the reality of the toy, in much the same way that *Cabbage Patch Kids* do. *Gremlins* are not alive; they are just toys. Besides, what parent would really want their child to be playing with such "demonic-looking" creatures at night. This is sure to cause nightmares for many children.

These images connected with *Gremlins* do not have a

basis in Christianity. In fact, Prophet Isaiah tells us, *And all thy children shall be taught of the Lord; and great shall be the peace of thy children.*[29] On the contrary, these images are filled with turmoil, not peace. They imply that if any of the rules are broken, havoc will break out. Is that peace?

Lucasfilm Ltd. will be premiering two new movies: *Labyrinth* and *Howard the Duck.* Both of these releases will be accompanied by a major roll-out of children's and juvenile products. *Labyrinth* will be highly visible in the toy stores. The film stars 80 different Henson-designed puppet/creatures, many of which are demonic-looking. As in the past, it is highly likely that toys will be made in the likenesses of these puppet/creatures. Rock idol *David Bowie* will be starring in *Labyrinth,* as well as writing and performing much of the music. In one promotional poster, *Bowie* is seen looking into a crystal ball, which is used in necromancy—communication with the dead. In addition, the new *Care Bears Movie II: A New Generation,* most likely will spawn new toys. It was in the first *Care Bears* movie that *Care Bear Cousins* were introduced.

Besides the mass influx of toys into the market corresponding with these blockbuster movies, there is another phenomenon. These films have become the "standard bearers of a new wave of fantasy/escape-oriented movies which have literally lifted the American film industry out of its financial depression."[30] Furthermore, these films express the desire to be released from something oppressive, such as personal failure and economic pressures. These films also appeal to the desire for adventure, a desire to find significance in everyday activities of life. Audiences love the thought that their mundane lives can be altered by invisible, but benign forces.[31]

What these movies do not teach is that none of these fantasies are reality. In this manner, they can become a source of frustration for many fantasy fans. In fact, it is only through the power of Jesus Christ that this fantasy can come true. Nevertheless, as the realities of life grow grimmer, the need for more fantasies become greater. It seems that the most successful films are those that provide the most convincing illusion of beneficient future societies where men can act like demi-gods. *Moviegoers constantly consume fantasies of a transcendent good that promises to save the world from destruction, and replaces order into chaotic lives.*[32]

Fantasies do have a place in our lives. But, they are like a double-edged knife. They can be dangerous if not used properly. Children should be encouraged to engage in fantasy play, but not to the extent that fantasy becomes the preferred world—over reality. Although demons are prevalent in many fantasy movies and corresponding toys, it is important that children know demons are real. However, they are not cute and friendly as Satan would have us believe. Children should be warned there is a war going on between Satan's battle for control of the world and Jesus. The Bible warns, *My people are destroyed for lack of knowledge: because thou hast rejected knowledge, I will also reject thee, that thou shalt be no priest to me: seeing thou hast forgotten the law of thy God, I will also forget thy children.*[33]

Peter warns in I Peter 5:8 that Satan walks the earth like a roaring lion seeking those he may devour. He seeks those who are not strong in their faith of Jesus Christ; he seeks those who hold a fascination for these movies and toys with occult images.

Children should be taught to battle the enemy, not with the "Force," but with God's weapons of warfare: prayer, praise, worship, the Word of God, the Name of Jesus, and the Blood of Jesus. In Ephesians 6:11, Paul tells us to wear the armor of God so that we will stand firm in battle against the devil. Children should also be taught to do this.

Today's children face a host of occult influences, from television to school books. It is important that they are aware of the tricks that Satan will use to deceive them, such as through "cute alien toys." But, it all begins with the parents. You must first be disciplined in your walk with the Lord in order to teach your child God's principles.

13

MONKEY SEE, MONKEY DO

Don't do as I do, do as I say. Although most parents would not verbalize this statement, many are saying it by their actions. Most children do not understand the logic behind this phrase; yet, they know to obey when these words are spoken by Mother or Father.

What about the *electronic parent*? Does television have the same authority over children that parents do? We know television teaches children. But, can it control their behavior? Can television networks show scenes of violence, hour after hour, and expect children not to imitate them? This is a major problem today. On television, acts of aggression rarely show consequences. As a result, children get a false impression of violence, leading many to imitate the aggressive acts.

But, children do not only imitate crimes such as burglary. Many also get ideas for suicides and murders from television.

In the March 1986 *Journal* of the National Federation for Decency, concern for this problem mounts as it is told of a murder-suicide that could have been influenced by television.

In Spanaway, Washington, the recent suicide of a ninth grade girl has led school authorities and teachers to question television's influence on children.

The suicide victim, who was an honor student and a member of the school's "gifted" program, apparently shot and killed two fellow students before killing herself. Authorities say the suicide victim had never been a discipline problem before.

Teachers are now trying to make sense of the incident. "We're trying to see if we can learn anything positive out of this . . ." said one teacher. Teachers expressed concern about the influence television has on students at junior high school age.

"We always see people on TV acting out their feelings," the teacher said. "It's TV that has become a model for our kids. People don't die on television, they just get shot."[1]

For this reason, many parents have become disillusioned with television and concerned about the effects of television violence on children. Violence and injuries often are not presented in an accurate manner. Many times, the injured person does not get hurt very badly. This problem is aggravated by the fact that, in many cases, those injured on television do not die; they just get shot. Television producers often lessen the severity of consequences from violent acts to meet network standards.

Regulations dictate the amount of bloodshed that can be shown on television. As a result, many injuries do not appear to be as harmful as they would be in reality. Many times, characters are shot in the head, only to have a small pool of blood form beside him. If this same act were committed in real life, there would be massive amounts of blood pouring from the wound. Since children believe what they see on television is true, they do not fully comprehend the consequences of shooting someone.

The same idea can be applied to shows like *Batman*, which focuses on the efforts of *Batman* and *Robin* fighting the *bad guys*. Every episode is filled with fight scenes. With each punch, large, colored words, such as *POW* and *SOCKO,* written in the form of a lightning bolt, flash on the television screen. Although these scenes are repeated throughout the show, no one is ever seen seriously injured. Many times, the *bad guys* are hit with such force that they become unconscious. In this manner, the show *does* portray consequences for acts of aggression. However, characters fall into unconsciousness in a comical manner. Some become cross-eyed and then fall backwards, with their feet flying high into the air. Others see stars and hear birds tweeting. In reality, if a person were hit with enough force to be rendered unconscious, extensive damage, both internally and externally, would have been done. Television does not show this. Generally, characters appear barely bruised. This confuses the child when he repeats the fight sequences the next day with his friend on the playground, and they both go home with black eyes and bloody noses.

There are dozens of other shows, both animated and not, which are filled with extensive violence. In the *Roadrunner* cartoon, a favorite cartoon among very young children, violent acts are presented constantly. The plot revolves around *Coyote's* efforts to catch the *Roadrunner*—always to no avail. Often, *Coyote* comes close, only to be stopped at the last minute. *Coyote,* portrayed as the bad guy, is blown to bits by explosions several times in one show. In addition, he falls off cliffs, is run over by trains, and has huge rocks fall on him. Amazingly, he never dies. He may be flattened, making him only a few inches tall, but, in the next scene, he appears as if nothing ever happened. The inference can be made that *Coyote* is given new life in every scene. He comes back to life, looking normal, after just being "destroyed." On the other hand, *Roadrunner,* portrayed as the *good guy,* is never hurt. He always escapes the *bad guy.* Because children view television as reality, how can we expect them to understand that violence can have lasting, damaging effects to others, possibly even lethal?

Prime-time television, geared for older age groups, also has its fill of shows portraying that *good guys* always win without getting hurt. The best example of this type of show is *A-Team*. This series portrays four *good guys* who battle a new set of *bad guys* each week. In the typical show, there is at least one car accident, in which the car flips over; no one is ever injured. The *good guys* and *bad guys* fight with automatic machine guns, grenades and other explosives. The worst that ever happens, however, is someone is knocked to the ground because of the force of an explosion. Rarely is anyone actually hit by a bullet, and they never die. With machine guns, this is hard to believe, especially when the fighting takes place within 100 feet of both sides. Nevertheless, with television, anything is possible—or so it seems.

Although I do not think *He-Man and Masters of the Universe* is an acceptable cartoon series for children, many parents disagree, on the basis of one point. One mother told a reporter that she liked *He-Man* because each violent act shows a consequence. "I don't like most cartoons, because not only are they violent, they don't show consequences. But, when (*He-Man* shows violence), it shows consequences," she said. "If he gets hit on the jaw, *He-Man* says, 'Boy, that hurt. I should try something different next time.'"[2]

More often than not, children are subjected to hour after hour of violence without seeing accurate consequences. True, TV criminals often go to jail for committing crimes, but their punishments are lessened when they plea bargain. The message the child learns: it is often "worth it" to commit a crime because the end punishment is less than the gain from the crime. On television, crime and violence are glorified. Those committing the acts of aggression are seen as "tough and cool." Characters, like *Mr. T*, often are congratulated for their actions. Children grow up wanting to be "cool." They grow up idolizing and imitating certain characters, such as *Rambo* and *Mr. T.* These characters are aggressive; so, the child acts aggressively. The child believes the behavior is OK because it was OK on television.

Because children watch 22–26 hours of television each week, these violent images are bound to affect them. In today's increasingly upwardly-mobile society, children are learning more from television because they are spending more time watching it than being in contact with any other person. As a result, they are embracing the ideals set forth by the *electronic parent,* which are not necessarily those that most adults would condone.

The *electronic parent* is not all bad, however. It is a good teaching tool. Like any other "good thing," if abused, television viewing can be detrimental to a child's social adjustibility and development. It has been estimated that a child will see 18,000 killings on television before graduating from high school. Are these lessons we want our children to learn? Parents can change this statistic by using video players. With videos, parents can preview certain shows; decide which ones are acceptable for their children, and tape them for the children to watch later.

To understand the effects television violence has on children and how it relates to adult crime, consider this: adults, especially those under pressure, often deal with problems in one of two ways—run or fight. Both of these are child-like behaviors. Adults should handle difficulties with logic and reason, not aggression. On the other hand, television teaches children to act on their feelings. If a character is attacked, he attacks back. Rarely is a "tough, good guy" seen discussing a problem. Most dilemmas are solved with force—swords and guns. Children, like characters on television, also fight back when attacked. Most children have not learned the art of using logic to solve problems. In addition, children learn behaviors from their environment, namely television and parents. If dilemmas are solved with force on television, children are apt to believe that this is the "correct way."

Many studies have attempted to show links between childhood television viewing and adult crimes. The results of the most extensive study done on this subject are as follows:

> The most extensive study ever done on TV violence shows a definite correlation between childhood viewing and an increase in adult crime. A 22-year study done by Rowell Huesmann Ph.D. and Leonard Eron Ph.D., professors of psychology at the University of Illinois at Chicago, surveyed the viewing habits of the entire third-grade class in one New York county. The two then reviewed the class at age 30.
>
> Of those with criminal records, the ones who had watched more TV violence as children were convicted as adults of crimes significantly more violent that others from the same classrooms. "Children who watch more violence on television learn to behave more aggressively," Dr. Huesmann said. "And they are likely to carry this behavior into adult life."
>
> The study also found that girls who watched more television violence than their peers grew up to punish their own children more harshly. However, Dr. Huesmann would not say that television violence was the sole factor responsible.[3]

Sadly, many children do not wait until they grow up to commit crimes. Many get ideas for crimes from television and commit them at very young ages. Another problem: TV criminals often are not caught. Therefore, children believe that they also will get away with a crime if they repeat it in detail. Consider this news account:

> In the Sepulveda district of San Fernando Valley recently, a 9-year-old burglary suspect became stuck in the chimney of a house.
>
> Police said the boy and a second 9-year-old are suspects in at least 10 burglaries in the neighborhood.
>
> Police also said that the idea of a chimney entrance was taken from a recent television show.[4]

It is children like these who are most likely to commit more crimes, possibly those that are more violent, when an adult.

Play and television help children learn and understand about the world. Unfortunately, television distorts reality—unbeknowing to the child. Television shows a world that is viewed from "Sunset Boulevard" spectacles. In this fantasy world—albeit viewed as reality—crime is rampant and sex ubiquitous. Success is effortless and all of life's problems are solved between commercials.

Despite these facts, and despite the countless studies that have been done on the subject, no conclusive theories have been found on whether or not television violence leads to adult crime. For many experts, the conclusion is clear: television violence produces aggressive behavior. Others disagree saying the evidence is far from definitive. Still, there are others who believe that watching violence on television can actually reduce direct aggressive behavior of the viewer. This "catharsis" theory dates back to Aristotle.[5] *Nevertheless, evidence does prove that television can be an exacerbating influence on children who are already prone to violence.*

What type of child is prone to violence? These are children who have suffered from neglect or abuse most of their lives.[6] These children also are more likely to spend most of their free time watching television. Most likely, these children live in poverty, and will grow up facing more frustrating poverty. Social scientists believe poverty is harder to bear today than in the past. Television and society have promised Americans so much; television always focuses on characters who achieve the "American Dream," effortlessly. This causes frustrations for those who do not reach the "American Dream."

They feel as if they have been cheated. They feel as if television, which they view as "reality," has lied to them. Children in these situations realize at an early age that they

167

most likely will never be able to "enter the successful, free-spending "establishment" that is pictured on television. As a result, they become frustrated, angry, expressing their feelings in aggressive, violent behavior.[7]

Children in these situations also lose respect for adults and other authority figures. Television teaches children that the things that count the most in society are securing money, status and success. However, these children see that their parents are poor, thus, not worthy of respect. When children do not respect their parents, it is difficult for them to learn to respect other authority figures. This leads to rebellion. The most common manifestation of rebellion is violence and aggression.

From these attitudes, a new kind of violence has been created and is rampantly growing in our neighborhoods. These are not muggings for the sake of money. These are **assaults for the sake of assault.** These are often referred to as senseless crimes.[8] Most experts have difficulty understanding these crimes. The only explanations: the child committing the crime feels as if he has nothing in common with the victim, or the child has failed to develop a basic sense of identity as a human being.

Charles E. Silberman discusses senseless crimes in his book *Criminal Violence, Criminal Justice*. He tells of three boys, 12 and 13 years old, who first set fire to a cat and then murdered a sleeping derelict by dousing him with lighter fluid and setting him on fire. The author writes: "The absence of affect (in the boys) is the most frightening aspect of all. In the past, juveniles who exploded into violence tended to feel considerable guilt or remorse afterward; the new criminals have been so brutalized in their upbringing that they seem incapable of viewing victims as fellow human beings, or of realizing that they have killed another person."[9]

Although poverty always has tended to breed violence and aggression, it has been only recently that violence has become "motiveless." Mounting frustrations in children's lives have led to shattered hopes and dreams, rage, and finally violence.

Although it cannot be proven that television violence directly causes adult crimes, we know that television is a powerful influence in a child's life. Thus, if a child is bombarded with violent scenes, the chances are greater that he will regress to aggression, rather than using logic to solve problems. Remember, children do imitate what they see. Especially if these behaviors are regarded as "cool" among his peers.

14

WHERE DO WE GO FROM HERE?

My position concerning toys and cartoons did not come because I was of a fanatical nature. It came because the voice of the Lord spoke to me and I listened to that voice. Nevertheless, I did not run right out and start proclaiming, "The Lord said that toys are bad!" Instead, I researched the subject and slowly the revelation came. The more I researched, the more I saw the "tentacles" tying to different subjects. My thinking continued to change and become solidified as a result of research. *One thing I try never to do in my presentations on toys and cartoons is speculate. I cannot speculate. I need facts.*

I want to know what toys and cartoons are actually doing to children today. But I do not spend all my time just researching. I spend a lot of time talking with families. I want to hear what they are saying. I want to understand them.

I believe there are many children in the church today who are accepting *He-Man, She-Ra* and toys like that, as God. Television and toys teach children that *He-Man* is the most powerful man in the universe. Sadly, many of these children are not given spiritual guidance to know otherwise. Often, parents do not take time to watch cartoons. They do not know the importance of the cartoons. Furthermore, they see toys as "cute" and therefore do not worry about them. In their opinion, if it looks good on the surface, then it is OK.

Often, parents are not disciplined in their own television viewing habits. If you do not discipline yourself, how can you discipline your children? Many mothers spend hours in front of television, watching soap operas, which has just as negative effect as toys and cartoons have on children. One of the greatest reasons God gave us children is so that we would feel a sense of responsibility.

When I talk to parents and children about toys and cartoons, I do not lay out dogma—"this is the way you have to train your children: 1,2,3,4,5." I lay out principles and information. Then, I leave the decision to parents to enact in their families. I let the Lord deal with their hearts about it. Many times, parents ask, "How am I going to put this in action in my family?" Let me assure you, I do not have toy burnings! It takes time to deal with a child. It is not just the child's decision. It is not just the parents' decision. It takes the working of the Holy Spirit to bring about the changes.

I have seen children bring bags of toys to services and put them at the altar and receive real spiritual victory. But, I do not encourage that. If you have been allowing your children to play with occult-oriented toys and watch shows filled with violence and the occult, and then you suddenly change your mind . . . it is going to take some time to say, "Hey, Mom and Dad made a mistake."

Although parents should monitor the toys that their children play with, they should remember that these are *children,* not short adults. I do not think it is right to make children the salt of the earth. *We* are the salt of the earth. Our young children are too tender of an age to be forced into being a "missionary." If they take the initiative to reach out to others—that is fine. But, we should not place our children in situations where they have to make those tough decisions.

Because children learn to be flexible and controlled by their peer groups, we need to make their peer group conform as close to our own teaching and values as possible. It is OK to allow your children to play in the neighborhood. However, I would discourage my child from spending the night at someone's house where the parents or guardians are not Christians. Don't misunderstand. I would open up my house anytime to non-Christian children; there, I could supervise. In my home, I would be the controlling factor, and we could be a witness, as a family, for the Lord. How much of a witness can a four or five-year-old be when he is in a situation where he is being controlled?

When a parent controls the toys his child plays with, he is not trying to turn the child into the "salt of the earth." Instead, he is guiding his child, helping him avoid "pits" that Satan has dug. Controlling a child's play time is rather simple.

If the child is young, take away the questionable toys and replace them with other toys. It is very important to give the child an "alternative toy." I believe in good toys for children, such as amoral and Christian toys. *Toys are necessary. They are an important part of development, an important part of life.*

If the child is older, parents should sit down with him or her and refer to *Webster's Dictionary* and the Bible. Look up Deuteronomy 18:9–12. Read those verses; then, have your child look up the words in the dictionary. Discuss the meanings of those words. Then, turn on the television to cartoons your child enjoys. Explain what is happening on the cartoons, and how those actions correspond to the practices outlined in Deuteronomy.

The following **Twelve Forbidden Practices** should be carefully studied by parents, grandparents and those concerned with the protection and growth of children. After studying them, watch the cartoons your children are watching. You will be appalled at what you see. You will be moved to seek the Lord on behalf of our little ones.

TWELVE FORBIDDEN PRACTICES

1. **Enchantments**
   The act of influencing by charms and incantations the practice of magical arts.

   Enchanter
   Sorcerer, magician, one who uses the human voice or music to bring another person under psychic control.
   Leviticus 19:26
   Deuteronomy 18:10-12
   II Chronicles 33:6
   II Kings 17:17
   Isaiah 47:8-11
   Jeremiah 27:8
   Daniel 1:20

2. **Witchcraft**
   The practice of dealing with evil spirits, the use of sorcery or magic.
   Deuteronomy 18:10-12
   II Chronicles 33:6
   I Samuel 15:23
   Galatians 5:19-21

3. **Sorcery**
   The use of power gained from the assistance or control of evil spirits, especially for divining.
   Jeremiah 27:9
   Isaiah 47:9
   Revelations 21:8

4. **Divination**
   Fortune-telling.
   Deuteronomy 18:10-14
   II Kings 17:17
   Jeremiah 27:8-9
   Jeremiah 29:8-9
   Acts 16:16-24

5. **Wizardry**
   The art of practices of a wizard; sorcery.

   Wizard
   One skilled in magic; sorcerer; male witch (to destroy in Israel).
   > Deuteronomy 18:11
   > II Kings 17:17
   > Exodus 22:18

6. **Necromancy**
   Communication with the dead; conjuration of the spirits of the dead for purposes of magically revealing the future or influencing the course of events.
   > Deuteronomy 18:11
   > I Samuel 28:1-25
   > Isaiah 8:19
   > I Chronicles 10:13-14

7. **Charm**
   Put a spell upon someone; to affect by magic.
   > Deuteronomy 18:11
   > Isaiah 19:3

8. **Star Gazing/Astrology**
   The divination of the supposed influence of the stars upon human affairs and terrestrial events by their positions and aspects.
   > Isaiah 47:12-15
   > Jeremiah 10:2
   > Daniel 1:18-20
   > Daniel 2:1-49
   > Daniel 4:1-37
   > Daniel 5:7-15

9. **Soothsaying**
   The act of foretelling events; prophesying by a spirit other than the Holy Spirit.
   > Joshua 13:22
   > Micah 5:12-15
   > Acts 16:16-18

10. **Prognostication**
    To foretell from signs or symptoms; prophesying without the Holy Spirit; soothsaying.
    > Isaiah 47:12-15
    > Joshua 13:22
    > Micah 5:12-15
    > Acts 16:16-18

11. **Observing Times**
    Astrology.
    > Leviticus 19:26
    > Deuteronomy 18:10-14
    > II Kings 21:6
    > II Chronicles 33:6

12. **Magic**
    Witchcraft.
    > Deuteronomy 18:10-12
    > II Chronicles 33:6
    > I Samuel 15:23

Also, search out other books that might be helpful. Tim LaHay's *Battle for the Mind* is an excellent book that will give an overview of the media.

It would be wise for parents to understand the *New Age Movement,* and how it affects what is being taught in schools. Parents should collect the knowledge necessary to combat the Humanistic influences in our society, which is being manifested by occultism. Many toys designed today reflect these occult ideals. Parents should know enough about the *New Age Movement* to understand that when their children come home and say they had to write a paper on "death," that this is a Humanistic way of *values clarification.* Schools should not be focusing on death, especially at the younger grade levels. Some schools even have sixth graders write their own wills and suicide notes. This is secular Humanistic education. *What Are They Teaching Our Children,* by Mel and Norma Gabler, is an excellent book that discusses the Humanistic teachings that are being presented in schools today.

Constance Cumbey discusses the *New Age Movement* in her book, *The Hidden Dangers of the Rainbow.*[1] Cumbey asserts that the "*New Age Movement* is a religion which closely parallels all the pagan traditions of the world. It is a counterfeit of Christian doctrine." Some of the movement's tenets include: belief in a central spiritual being known as the *Source* or the *God of Force;* belief in the *divinity of man;* belief in the *Law of Rebirth,* also known as *reincarnation;* belief that God is inferior to something known as the *Solar Logos;* belief in *evolution;* belief in *salvation by initiation and works* rather than by atonement and grace; and belief in the existence of *masters* and of an occult hierarchy.[2] For years, schools have been teaching many of these tenets, especially evolution.

When parents discover what their children are learning, they begin to question the value of public school education.

People often ask me about Christian schools versus public schools. If parents want to send their children to a Christian school, they should make sure the school is really good. Not only good educationally, but that it teaches Godly concepts. The teachers should be really "turned on" to the Lord. There is nothing better than a good Christian school. But, there is nothing worse than a bad Christian school. I know from my own experiences, that a child cannot go to a public school without being affected by it. Some children can go to a public school and still come out OK. In fact, I have a friend who goes to Princeton, where he is bombarded with Humanism. Yet, he has a tremendous relationship with the Lord. Nevertheless, I know he feels the effects of that teaching.

You may say, "we live in a good community so the public school is good." Remember, for the past 100 years teachers have been taught Humanism. Consequently, Christian teachers in public school teach Humanism without realizing it.

Public school, for the most part, teaches that we should be like everyone else, to be a part of the whole. In reality, your child should be taught to be an individual. God created him an individual. Part of the *Body of Christ* has suffered from this because they, too, try to make everybody exactly alike. I call them the *cookie cutter Christians. They have a "set mold" and tell you this is what a Christian is supposed to be. But, God uses sand paper, not a "mold," to make an individual creation. He puts in us the necessary abilities and talents to do His will. The only way we will find fulfillment is to do His will.*

If we follow God's will, we will not fit into the mold of a *cookie cutter Christian.* Instead, we will be the individual who He wants us to be. Throughout my ministry, I have always tried to follow God's will and not be like everyone else. I am a very "laid back" person, although I feel as comfortable in a suit or tuxedo as I do in jeans. There are not many people like that. Still, I reveal my individuality in a different way than wearing a Hawaiian shirt on the pupit like one minister I admire. However, there are times when I do feel like doing that. *The "tie" is not "Samson's Hair."* Some people think if we take off the tie we lose God's "annointing." This is not true!

Children should strive to be individuals, and not be like Joey and Suzy, next door. Television fosters this idea of being like everyone else. Children want every toy advertised because "everyone else already has it." As a result, television makes certain toys, which Christians would find unacceptable, appear very attractive. Many times, the ads even convince parents that the toys are "harmless and cute." In the end, Satan wins. He gets a hold on the child and his imagination.

Wouldn't it be a better solution to this problem to go from pacifism to an active understanding of the effects that media and other influences are having upon our lives?

MY CONCLUSION

I do not assume that all people are wrong; nevertheless, I do realize many are being deceived. My assumption is that they are "perishing for the lack of knowledge." God led me into this ministry so I could make parents **aware** of the danger behind certain television programs and toys. My purpose is to *inform, not condemn.*

I want to stress that **television, in and of itself, is not intrinsically wrong!** The bad influences from television are fostered by abusive viewing habits and the philosophy of "no absolutes" by writers and producers of television programming. If television viewing is going to be allowed in the home, the following steps should be taken to safeguard the children.

(1) **Know what your children are watching.**

Parents will have to sacrifice part of their time to do this. But it is important. Parents should be aware of what their children are watching. Television should not be a babysitter.

(2) **Discuss values, plots and behaviors seen on TV with your children.**

Children cannot always draw accurate conclusions from what they see. It is important for parents to explain the difference between what is shown and reality.

(3) **Plan TV watching.**

Television should not be turned on for background noise. Determine what shows would be suitable for your family and watch only those. This lessens the risk that children will be exposed to negative influences.

(4) **Take responsibility as a parent.**

Parents should be firm with children regarding certain shows. Just because Stevie's mom lets him watch a certain show does not mean your child should watch it. If you do not think a show is suitable, don't allow your child to watch it.

These same principles can and should be applied to toys. Be aware of what toys they play with and the possible effects that they can have on the child. If a toy does not agree with your understanding of God's Word, explain your feelings to the child. Let him know why you do not want him to play with the toy. This way, he, too, will be taking part in the decision making process.

In his latest book, *Put the Trumpet to Thy Mouth,* Rev. David Wilkerson suggests there should be an abolition of television from the home. "To see so many precious children of God desensitized and defensive about television honestly scares me. What kind of mystical hold does it have on this age?"[3] He gives an example of the hold that television had on one family.

"The headlines in a recent paper read, 'House Burns While Family Stays Glued to TV.' The whole family was so addicted, no one would leave to call the fire department.

"By the time a teenager is 18, he has watched an equivalent of six years of television and had only four months of church. And people tell me it's not an idol."[4]

Wilkerson continues, "In contrast, *how sad to see our Christian children prostrate on the floor in front of this hideous idol, eating and drinking in that which blinds them to the good and glorifies the bad.* We are raising spiritual cripples, warping tender minds, and sitting idly by as they drift into moral blindness. I can see no other reason for Christ's prophecy that 'Children shall rise up against their parents, and shall cause them to be put to death,'[5] other than our having turned them into monsters with no tenderness or compassion. *Television is doing just that—monsterizing our children.*"[6]

Some people believe this position is extreme. Although some Christian families would view this unthinkable, I only have seen families benefit by the removal of television from the home. Follow God's Word and pray for discernment regarding toys and shows. *If fasting from food awakens our spirit to the voice of the Lord, then wouldn't a fast from television be just as valid?* Those who are least likely to remove the television or enact guidelines for it are the ones who need to most.

THE ALTERNATIVE

Because these changes will not come overnight, especially for older children, it is important to have alternatives. Alternatives help lessen the severity of change. This also will keep the child from getting bored. I will quickly outline my suggested alternatives, and then discuss them:

(1) **A television fast**
This should be done for whatever length of time you think is necessary. I would recommend that it be done at least once a year.

(2) **Video tape recorder**
   You can buy video players for about $200.
(3) **Preview a TV show**
   You may wish to record it and show it later to your children.
(4) **Bible videos and Christian music videos**
(5) **Build a video library**
   Children's video tapes are less expensive than those for adults. If you are more affluent, buy a monitor (a TV without channels) and a video player. This way, whenever your child wants to watch television, he can choose any video you own and have already approved.

Videos are ideal for children. They like watching the same shows over and over again. Whereas, an adult tires of a show after seeing it two or three times, children will watch a video tape dozens of times.

The same is true of children's books. Children enjoy hearing the same, familiar material read to them over and over again. Most children have three or four favorite books of which they never seem to tire. I remember when I was a child, my favorite book was *Cowboy Andy*. He was a little child who lived in the city. He got on a train to go visit his uncle on a ranch out West. There, he learned all about a ranch. My Mom read that and also *Green Eggs and Ham* to me so many times as we traveled in the car to places where my Dad would preach. Mom and Dad would get so tired of *Cowboy Andy* and *Green Eggs and Ham* that Mom would sometimes hide the books. Sooner or later, I would find them and she would have to read them a dozen or more times. Then, she would hide them again.

If you are going to have television in your home, I think the best alternative is the video player. If a monitor is too expensive, just pull off the knobs from the television set, or buy a television set with a channel lock on it. That way, even if you are not at home, you still are exerting some control over your child's television viewing. Another good thing about video players: you can erase unsuitable scenes from shows that otherwise would be acceptable for your child.

It is time parents, and anyone concerned about children, take action to protect today's youth. ***This generation is being deceived by the "master of deception." Unless we do something about it, children will grow up with more of a foundation in the occult, than in the power of Jesus.***

Although the solution to this ever-increasing problem starts in the home, it does not stop there. We should let those responsible for making these occult toys and violent shows know that we will not tolerate them. Letters have a strong impact on companies, and I strongly encourage you to write toy companies, toy stores and television networks to voice your opinion.

Letters are not all that is needed. When writing to toy stores, enclose copies of sales receipts from the last few months to show them that you do patronize their store. Let them know you disapprove of the type of toys they are selling. Tell the store manager you are not alone in your opinion. Then, encourage others to do the same. Remember, it takes team effort to achieve any goal. It takes even more team effort when dealing with Satan.

Remember, the battle is the Lord's. With His help and guidance, we will defeat Satan, and prevent another ***turmoil in the toy box.***

BIBLIOGRAPHY

CHAPTER THREE
1. Dager, Albert J., "Playing with Danger: Some Popular Toys Analyzed," *Media Spotlight,* 1985.
2. Finley, Kathy and Mitch Finley, "Nurturing Your Imagination," *Marriage and Family Living,* 1982.
3. Ibid.
4. Matterson, E.M., *Play and Playthings for the Preschool Child,* Penguin Books Inc., New York, 1965.
5. Pratney, Winkie, *Mindfixing is an Addiction of the '80s,* March 1983.
6. Finley and Finley, 1982.
7. Allen, Audrianna and Elizabeth Neterer, "Guide for the Selection of Toys," *Play—Children's Business,* Association for Childhood Education International, Washington, D.C., 1963, pp. 14-26.
8. Sutton-Smith, Brian, "Ambivalence in Toyland," *Natural History,* December 1985, pp. 6, 8, 10.
9. Ibid.
10. Ibid.
11. Finley and Finley, 1982.

CHAPTER FOUR
1. Allen, Audrianna and Elizabeth Neterer, "Guide for the Selection of Toys," *Play—Children's Business,* Association for Childhood Education International, Washington, D.C., 1963, pp. 14-26.
2. Frank, Lawrence K., "Play and Child Development," *Play—Children's Business,* 1963, pp. 4-6.
3. Kawin, Ethel, *The Wise Choice of Toys,* University of Chicago, 1934.
4. Ibid.
5. Ibid.
6. Feeney, Stephanie and Marion Magarick, "Choosing Good Toys for Children," *Young Children,* vol. 40, no. 1, November 1984, pp. 21-25.
7. Kawin, 1934.
8. Allen and Neterer, 1963.

9. Piers, Maria and Genevieve Millet Landau, *The Gift of Child's Play*, Walker and Co., New York, 1980.
10. Ibid.
11. Ibid.
12. Ibid.
13. Ibid.

CHAPTER FIVE
1. Sutton-Smith, Brian, "Ambivalence in Toyland," *Natural History*, December 1985, pp. 6, 8, 10.
2. Ibid.
3. Ibid.
4. Ibid.
5. Ibid.
6. Ibid.
7. Dager, Albert J., "Playing with Danger: Some Popular Toys Analyzed," *Media Spotlight*, 1985.
8. Ibid.
9. Wildmon, Donald, *The Home Invaders*, SP Publications, Wheaton, Ill., 1985.
10. Buscaglia, Leo, *Toys Can Mean So Much More than Child's Play*, distributed by Special Features Syndication, Feb. 24, 1985.
11. Ibid.
12. *The Hume Moneyletter*, "Toys and Even Better Play," April 24, 1985.
13. Ibid.
14. Ibid.
15. Ibid.
16. Sutton-Smith, 1985.
17. Dager, 1985.
18. Buscaglia, 1985.

CHAPTER SIX
1. Esteves, Roland, "Children's TV: A Guide for Parents," *Marriage and Family Living*, January 1982, pp. 14-15.
2. Ibid.
3. Kawin, 1934.
4. Winn, Marie, *The Plug-In Drug*, Viking, New York, 1977.
5. Ibid.

6. Ibid.
7. Finley and Finley, 1982.
8. Winn, 1977.
9. Ibid.
10. Finley and Finley, 1982.
11. Piers and Landau, 1980.
12. Ibid.
13. Healy, Michelle, "TV for Kids: Up to Two Hours a Day OK," *USA Today,* February 11, 1986, p. 1.
14. Piers and Landau, 1980.
15. Ibid.
16. Ibid.
17. Ibid.
18. Ibid.
19. Esteves, 1982.
20. Ibid.
21. Dager, 1985.
22. Ibid.
23. Ibid.
24. Finley and Finley, 1982.

CHAPTER SEVEN
1. "Cabbage Patch Vitamin Ad is Subject of ACT Complaint," *Toy and Hobby World,* February 1986, p. 25.
2. Ibid.
3. "Children's Cartoons Designed to Sell Kids Toys," *The Detroit News*, November 10, 1985, p. 4E.
4. Ibid.
5. Ibid.
6. Ibid.
7. Ibid.
8. Ibid.
9. Sobel, Robert, "Syndicators Unleash Flood of First-Run Kid Products," *Television/Radio Age,* August 20, 1984, p. 33.
10. Ibid.
11. Ibid.
12. Ibid., p. 34.
13. Ibid.
14. Bishop, Pete, "Tragic Comedy: Animator Faults Quality and

Messages of Today's Saturday Morning Cartoons," *The Dallas Morning News,* June 8, 1985, p. 6F.
15. National Federation for Decency.
16. Thomas, Cal, reprinted with permission from the *Moral Majority Report,* radio broadcast, June 27, 1985.

CHAPTER EIGHT
1. Finley and Finley, 1982.
2. Buscaglia, 1985.
3. Venezia, Joyce. A., "Cabbage Patch Kids Get an Education," *Associated Press.*
4. Associated Press, "Is Your Cabbage Patch Kid Dirty? It's Time for Cabbage Patch Clinic," *Times Daily,* May 19, 1985.
5. Ibid.
6. Ibid.
7. "Barbie at 24: A Curse or Blessing?" *Newsweek.*
8. Ibid.
9. Vespa, Mary, *People,* book review, March 17, 1986, p. 23.
10. Freedman, Rita, *Beauty Bound,* Lexington Books, 1986.
11. "Barbie Dolls Mark Silver Anniversary," *The Dallas Morning News,* February 20, 1984, p. 3C.
12. Ibid.
13. *People,* March 17, 1986.
14. *The Dallas Morning News,* February 20, 1984.
15. Hamilton, Edith, *Mythology,* Little, Brown and Co., Boston, 1943, pp. 184-190.
16. Dager, Albert J., "The Unicorn: Fabled Beast of Myth and Magic," *Media Spotlight,* 1986.
17. Ibid.
18. Daniel 7:8.
19. Mark 12:28-34.
20. Dager, Albert J., "The Care Bears: Not Your Ordinary Yogi Bear," *Media Spotlight,* July-September, 1985, pp. 1, 3, 13, 16.
21. Ibid.
22. *Hallmark Properties,* information from a "Rainbow Brite" promotional poster.
23. Cumbey, Constance, *The Hidden Dangers of the Rainbow,* Huntington House, Inc., Shreveport, Louisiana, 1983.

CHAPTER NINE
1. Sobel, 1984.
2. New York Times News Service, "Little Boys Can't Get Enough of He-Man Dolls, TV Shows," *The Dallas Morning News,* December 22, 1984, p. 3C.
3. Ibid.
4. Ibid.
5. Ibid.
6. *Time,* January 7, 1985.
7. New York Times News Service, 1984.
8. Ibid.
9. "Toys 'R's," *Newsweek,* December 30, 1985, p. 65.
10. Cohn, Gary, *The Power of Point Dread,* Mattel, Inc., 1983.
11. Cohn, Gary, *The Magic Stealer,* Mattel, Inc., 1983, pp. 10-11.
12. Knorr, Bryce, *She-Ra, the Princess of Power,* Western Publishing Co., Inc., Racine, Wisconsin, 1985.
13. All information for the Glossary of Terms come from *He-Man* and *She-Ra* comic books, Mattel, Inc.

CHAPTER TEN
1. "Coalition on TV Violence Says War Toys Now the Most Popular," Religious News Service, July 16, 1985.
2. Ibid.
3. Ibid.
4. Dager, Albert J., "Playing with Danger: Some Popular Toys Analyzed," 1985.
5. Religious News Service, 1985.
6. Brothers, Dr. Joyce, "War Toys Set a Bad Example for Children Learning to Cope," *The Star-Ledger,* February 14, 1986, p. 74.
7. Ibid.
8. Ibid.
9. Ibid.
10. Dager, Albert J., "Playing with Danger: Some Popular Toys Analyzed," 1985.
11. Matthew 5:39.

CHAPTER ELEVEN
1. *D & D—Only a Game?,* Pro Family Forum, Fort Worth, Texas, 1981.

2. Heller, Jean, "Joys, Dangers of Game where One's Imagination is the Limit," *San Francisco Examiner and Chronicle*, September 23, 1979.

3. Ibid.

4. *Rolling Stone*, 1980.

5. Heller, 1979.

6. Ibid.

7. Ibid.

8. Ibid.

9. Oman, Anne H., "Dungeons and Dragons: It's Not Just a Game. It's an Adventure," *The Washington Post*, February 20, 1981, p. C2.

10. Heller, 1979.

11. Crichton, Doug, "Pair Blames Son's Suicide on Dungeons and Dragons," *Richmond Times-Dispatch*, August 11, 1983.

12. Associated Press, "Fantasy Games Find Fervid Fans," *Longview Morning Journal*, May 17, 1981, p. 8D.

13. *Model Retailer*, 1980.

14. "Dungeons and Dragons," *Cornerstone Magazine*, Chicago, Illinois, December 1980.

15. Ibid.

16. North, Dr. Gary, *None Dare Call It Witchcraft*.

17. Dekker, Rev. John, "Dungeons and Dragons: The Occult and Psychodrama," *Temple Times*, East Point, Georgia, November 1, 1981.

18. Pro Family Forum, 1981.

19. Deuteronomy 18:9-12.

20. Loohauis, Jackie, "Gurus of the Games," *The Milwaukee Journal*, November 19, 1981.

21. *D & D Handbook*, p. 7.

22. *Dungeon Masters Handbook*, p. 38.

23. Ibid.

24. Ibid., p. 39.

25. *Deities and Demigods Instruction Manaul*, p. 5.

26. *Dungeon Masters Guide*, p. 25.

27. *D & D Players Handbook*, p. 40.

28. *Dungeon Masters*, pp. 38-39.

29. *D & D Handbook*, p. 7.

30. *D & D Players Handbook*, p. 40.

31. *Dungeon Masters Guide*, p. 42.

32. *Players Handbook,* p. 20.
33. *Dungeon Master,* p. 229.
34. *Dungeon Masters Guide,* p. 86.
35. Matthew 5:28.
36. Christian Life Ministries, *Answers to Common Questions about Dungeons and Dragons,* 1981.
37. Ibid.
38. Ibid.
39. *Cornerstone Magazine,* December 1980.
40. Ephesians 5:15-16.
41. Dekker, 1981.
42. Ibid.
43. Ibid.
44. Psalm 23:4-6 RSV.

CHAPTER TWELVE

1. *Toy and Hobby World,* special advertising insert, February 1986.
2. Ibid.
3. Ibid.
4. Ibid.
5. Ibid.
6. Ibid.
7. Psalm 127:3 RSV.
8. Amendola, Rebecca, "More than Just a Pretty Face . . . " *Christ for the Nations,* January 1985.
9. Proverbs 22:6 RSV.
10. Hinson, Hal, "The Dark Side of Films for Kids," *USA Today.*
11. Ibid.
12. Ibid.
13. Ibid.
14. Ibid.
15. Ibid.
16. Ibid.
17. Amendola, 1985.
18. John 10:10 RSV.
19. Psalm 106:34-41 RSV.
20. Amendola, 1985.
21. Styll, John, "The Gospel of Lucas," *Contemporary Christian Magazine,* August 1983.

22. Ibid.
23. Ibid.
24. Ibid.
25. Ibid.
26. Ibid.
27. Amendola, 1985.
28. Ibid.
29. Isaiah 54:13.
30. Cushing, Kevin, "Escaping the Future?" *Contemporary Christian Magazine*, August 1983.
31. Ibid.
32. Ibid.
33. Hosea 4:6.

CHAPTER THIRTEEN
1. *Journal,* National Federation for Decency, March 1986.
2. New York Times News Service, December 22, 1984.
3. *Ladies Home Journal,* April 1985.
4. *Journal,* National Federation for Decency, March 1986.
5. Rubinstein, Eli A., "TV Violence: A Historical Perspective," *Children and Faces of Television,* 1981.
6. Piers and Landau, 1980.
7. Ibid.
8. Ibid.
9. Ibid.

CHAPTER FOURTEEN
1. Cumbey, 1983.
2. Ibid.
3. Wilkerson, David, *Set the Trumpet to Thy Mouth,* World Challenge, Inc., Lindale, Texas, 1985, p. 57.
4. Ibid., p. 66.
5. Mark 13:12.
6. Wilkerson, p. 67.

You read PHIL PHILLIPS' book ...now listen!

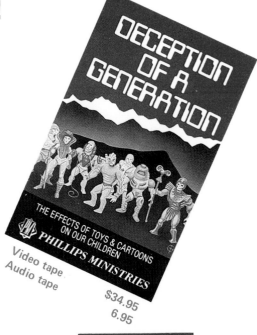

PLEASE NOTE: The advertising messages that follow have been placed by producers of alternative products.